"Having spent the past 25 years pursuing excellence in high technology industries, focusing on business development, strategic planning, venture growth, and scaling operations, being proactive in messaging and managing PR is absolutely a key success factor for all entrepreneurs and company executives. As an integral PR partner in a large-scale investment I led over 20 years ago, Roger's subject matter expertise is highly qualified."

Chris Arsenault, *Managing Partner, Inovia Capital*

"*The Communications Consultant's Master Plan* provides a solid bedrock for anyone getting into PR, particularly those starting their own agency. Roger has covered the bases in a way that's truly impressive. I wish this was around when I got started!"

Anthony Vagnoni, *President, Avagnoni Communications*

"A new epoch is here. It's time to make authentic, bold moves and manifest new realities. If you're serious about taking your career to the next level, Roger Darnell's expertise will guide you with vibrant light, illuminating your practice and revealing that it's so much more than PR – it's an experiential journey of breakthroughs and discoveries. Roger not only shows you the way, but he also goes there with you."

Jason White, *Experiential Director; former Co-Founder and Chief Creative Officer, Leviathan*

"Think of *The Communications Consultant's Master Plan* as a kind of hardware store for just about anyone seeking to get anyone else to buy or believe something. It's a comprehensive guide offering valuable nuts-and-bolts advice, assistance and support in realms such as public relations and investor relations. Especially useful are the action items offered after each chapter."

Stuart Elliott, *Panel Moderator/Speaker; former* New York Times *Advertising Columnist*

"For PR, marketing or communications professionals considering taking that first step into running a firm of their own, Roger Darnell offers a step-by-step, how-to guide from his nearly three-decade career serving as PR counsel for some of the nation's most well-known creative agencies. Full of real-world business lessons and high-level overviews of successful campaign strategies for different types of business clients, Roger provides the blueprint of success for the enterprising independent PR and communications professional to build a business that achieves professional rewards and personal freedom beyond what most traditional employees ever achieve. If success is a journey, and not just a destination, Roger makes for an engaging travel companion when you're ready to branch out on your own."

    G. Scott Shaw, *President and Founder, Everclear Marketing, Inc.*

"Years ago, I set out to only work with the best of the best, and Roger Darnell epitomizes that standard. As Chief PR Counsel for Cutters Studios since 2014, his impact on our organization's success is beyond measure. Roger is a true partner in every sense of the word. He really takes the time to get to know the culture and the spirit of the companies he represents. Roger's unique approach and clear strategy have been a guiding light for our company. He has become a part of us, and I can't imagine where we would be without him. For anyone wanting to know how to build similar expertise and apply it to allow themselves and everyone around them to soar, I have one suggestion: Read this book."

    Craig Duncan, *President/Managing Director, Cutters Studios*

"After more than 20 years as a professional colleague and friend, I've admired how Roger continues to adapt and apply his expertise to the evolutions in technology and media that drive new approaches to public relations. His kindness, integrity and approachability are key to his professional success, and also key to what makes *The Communications Consultant's Master Plan* so helpful. With this book and its Explorations, Roger shares practical ideas and best practices for implementing a public relations strategy to help elevate any new business initiative or career path."

    Karen Raz, *Owner, Raz Public Relations*

"Rich in details and comprehensive in scope, Roger Darnell provides beginning and seasoned professionals with everything they need to know for a successful career in the communications business."

Rebecca Bedrossian, *Global Content Director, Wunderman Thompson*

"In *The Communications Consultant's Master Plan*, Roger expertly breaks down the knowledge needed to build a PR business from the ground up, with both in-depth details on everything from writing contracts to finding new clients, in an engaging, friendly tone that makes this handbook approachable, informative and a joy to read. After diving into everything Roger has done so far in his career, I can't wait to see what he has planned for next."

Jacqueline Poole, *Senior Editor,*
Manager of Social Programs, Patrick Faller Media

"This is a well-rounded, heart-filled reference from an innate communications expert who understands the key to this business – community itself."

Angela Natividad, *Co-Founder, Hurrah Group;*
Editor, L'Atelier BNP Paribas; Writer; Advisor

"Who would have thought that great communications were so deeply rooted in the strategy and fabric of the target organization? Answer: Everyone who is great at it! Darnell has revealed where his magical body of work has come from – it comes from that systemic understanding of the organizations he is communicating about. We are lucky to have him share with us the wisdom he has gained and his 'tricks of the trade.' Thanks for making it easier to follow in your footsteps!"

Brett Knowles, *CEO, www.Hirebook.com*

"At all SHOOT platforms, Roger Darnell is well known as a top-tier PR pro. The many attributes that set him and his work apart certainly add up to the great benefit of his clients. This book is a viable means for training a new generation of highly skilled, independent communicators, and for entrepreneurs to see why adding professional PR counsel is a key to succeeding at the highest level."

Gerald Giannone, *Co-Owner, DCA Business Media LLC*

The Communications Consultant's Master Plan

This volume builds on Roger Darnell's *The Communications Consultant's Foundation* by providing insider knowledge gained over the past three decades atop the field of communications consulting, incorporating lessons learned serving businesses in the global creative industry.

Going beyond the basics of a communications consulting business, this book parses and distills the knowledge of top business management luminaries, helping readers build and expand their expertise to heighten their opportunities, and maximize all aspects and phases of their businesses, from start-up through to succession. It discusses essential topics including:

- The business of running a PR agency, with emphasis on landing clients and honing expertise to remain exceptional
- Advanced PR practices including investor relations and strategic planning
- Agency expansion, addressing growth and exit strategies

Working PR professionals, entrepreneurs, students, and recent graduates will appreciate high-level insights from a seasoned business owner, as well as templates for proposals, campaign planning, and more. Read with *The Communications Consultant's Foundation* or on its own, this book will lead readers on life-changing journeys and help a new generation of smart communicators take their professional pursuits to the highest levels.

Roger Darnell is an author, communications consultant, publisher, and speaker. Already central to billions of positive media impressions worldwide, his ambitious collaborations with entrepreneurs and media luminaries continue soaring to new heights.

The Communications Consultant's Master Plan

Leveraging Public Relations Expertise for Client and Personal Success

Roger Darnell

NEW YORK AND LONDON

Cover image: © Getty Images

First published 2022
by Routledge
605 Third Avenue, New York, NY 10158

and by Routledge
4 Park Square, Milton Park, Abingdon, Oxon, OX14 4RN

Routledge is an imprint of the Taylor & Francis Group, an informa business

© 2022 Roger Darnell

The right of Roger Darnell to be identified as author of this work has been asserted in accordance with sections 77 and 78 of the Copyright, Designs and Patents Act 1988.

All rights reserved. No part of this book may be reprinted or reproduced or utilised in any form or by any electronic, mechanical, or other means, now known or hereafter invented, including photocopying and recording, or in any information storage or retrieval system, without permission in writing from the publishers.

Trademark notice: Product or corporate names may be trademarks or registered trademarks, and are used only for identification and explanation without intent to infringe.

Library of Congress Cataloging-in-Publication Data
Names: Darnell, Roger, author.
Title: The communications consultant's master plan: leveraging public relations expertise for client and personal success / Roger Darnell.
Description: New York, NY : Routledge, 2022. | Includes bibliographical references and index.
Identifiers: LCCN 2021029298 (print) | LCCN 2021029299 (ebook) | ISBN 9781032012575 (hardback) | ISBN 9781032012599 (paperback) | ISBN 9781003177913 (ebook)
Subjects: LCSH: Public relations consultants. | Public relations.
Classification: LCC HD59. D2563 2022 (print) | LCC HD59 (ebook) | DDC 659.2023—dc23
LC record available at https://lccn.loc.gov/2021029298
LC ebook record available at https://lccn.loc.gov/2021029299

ISBN: 978-1-032-01257-5 (hbk)
ISBN: 978-1-032-01259-9 (pbk)
ISBN: 978-1-003-17791-3 (ebk)

DOI: 10.4324/9781003177913

Typeset in Goudy
by KnowledgeWorks Global Ltd.

For all those willing to work hard, where encouragement can lighten the load, and inside knowledge can revolutionize the world.

Dedicated to my better half Beth Darnell; my father, brother, daughter, and son; all our wonderful family members and friends; and to all the illustrious clients of The Darnell Works Agency, past and present.

I also wish to thank some of the many people who have reshaped my world through their kindness, support, and generosity. In addition to those already mentioned, I am also eternally grateful to Michael Terpin, Lisa Cleff-Kurtz, Ric Peralta, Simon Needham, James Sommerville, Will Travis, Britt Andreatta, Ph.D., David C. Baker, Randy Baker, Helena Bouchez, Deirdre K. Breakenridge, Bud Caddell, Gini Dietrich, Craig Duncan, Blair Enns, Craig Fischer, Ph.D., Michael W. Garfinkel, Gerald Giannone, Jennifer Handshew, Chad Hutson, Gaston Legorburu, Brett Knowles, Roger C. Martin, Shawn Pucknell, Karen Raz, Steven Masur, Matt Miller, Elise Mitchell, Michael Morrison, Meredith Norwich, Dean Ramser, Ed.D., Sari Rosen, Austin Shaw, G. Scott Shaw, Norm Smallwood, Mark Smiciklas, Tim Street, James E. Turner, M.D., Pamela Tuscany, John Walker, Angus Wall, Jason White, Judy Wolff, and all those whose works and deeds have inspired me to aim high, be all I can be, and do all I can do.

Contents

List of Figures	xiii
List of Tables	xiv
i Introduction	1
ii My Story	6
Part I PR Client Services	**9**
1 Winning and Managing PR Accounts	11
2 Client Positioning and Communications Strategy	30
3 Investors and Investor Relations	39
4 Advanced PR Account Management	49
5 Advanced Communications and Marketing Strategies and Tactics	73
Part II Agency Business	**89**
6 Agency Management	91
7 Professional Development	108
8 Scaling and Exit Strategies and Tactics	119
Part III PR Master Toolset	**131**
9 The Right Marketing Plan	133
10 Action Plans	142
11 The Art and Craft of Presentation	152

Appendices 167

    Sample Cover and Campaign Planning Letter   169

    Sample Proposal   171

    Sample Letter Agreement   181

    Sample Monthly Activity Report   184

Index   189

Figures

1	Phases of Org Growth	35
2	Media View Spectrum	52
3	Inverted Pyramid	55
4	The Experience Space	64
5	Client Strength Finder	75
6	Southwest Airlines Strategy Map	138
7	What Are Objectives and Key Results?	144
8	Shares of Communications	150

Tables

1	Internal Communications Initiatives	36
2	External Communications Initiatives	37
3	Strong Suits for HQ Strategy	76
4	Strong Suits for Steady Strategy	77
5	Strong Suits for Flush Strategy	79
6	Strong Suits for Maverick Strategy	80
7	Client Activity Organizer	148

i
Introduction

If you have been pursuing an interest in the field of Public Relations, you have an advantage over me at the time I started a PR firm, more than 20 years ago. In my case, it was a combination of knacks and talents – involving writing, communications, business, film, television, and the creative industry – as well as the standing need to find a job, that drove me onto this career superhighway.

Worth noting, PR was not my major in college; until recently I was never a member of an association focused exclusively on PR; and my agency is nowhere to be found in O'Dwyer's annual rankings of PR firms. Still, as a communications consultant specializing in the creative industry, and an entrepreneur, I have built a winning track record, where a good number of my remarkable colleagues around the globe consider me among the world's best at my job.

Perhaps you are familiar with the companion to this volume, The Communications Consultant's Foundation. There, true to its title, the full arena where business communications dissipate, fall, or rise is illuminated, and a paradigm for building personal and client success in this widely respected vocation is exhaustively laid out.

Throughout most of the time spent operating The Darnell Works Agency, I have diligently emphasized the optimization of business for my illustrious clientele. Frankly, I view this as the key ingredient in my professional prosperity. As a specialized writer with a strong business sense, and a deep commitment to providing invaluable, highly impactful service focusing on communications, I worked my way to a status that has proven to be much more rewarding than anything I imagined. Believe me, up until starting this venture, I spent a lot of time fantasizing about using my intelligence and interests to work independently, achieve financial security, and fulfill my career aspirations.

DOI: 10.4324/9781003177913-1

Several years ago, I was inspired to distill the knowledge and insights I have gained for others to use in expanding their career opportunities. Creating this curriculum has taken me in some new directions, requiring me to look beyond my clients' needs. While surveying some aspects of the PR field – and business in general – took me outside my first-hand experiences, by embracing the standard communications consulting role of <u>problem finder and solver</u>, and the mission-critical need to <u>always be learning</u>, some sage wisdom has been divined. I hope you will find it to be pivotal.

Naturally, I heartily recommend you read my introductory book, where the key skill set of this profession – Account Management, Customer Service, Planning, Writing, Media Relations, Measurement, and Reporting – is conveyed and contextualized within the principles of business communications. While the takeaways are encapsulated in these pages, your initial and long-term success is sure to rely on having the strongest possible foundation.

*

A great deal of self-confidence comes with the proven ability to handle strategic and promotional communications services according to specific objectives, and to produce results that add measurable value to an organization. For one example, imagine connecting with a colleague after she has changed jobs, and placing that news in *The New York Times*. This is the type of feat one might secure by earning a PR degree, working one's way up inside a PR firm or corporation to an account position, and contributing as part of a team. On the other hand, it could be accomplished through your own firm, according to your own terms, where you completely own the accolades and rewards.

Advancing the proficiency and application of our key skill set with a keen sense of what distinguishes healthy enterprises from others, and steering accordingly, we are going to prepare you to truly excel as an immensely powerful communications leader. By participating and advancing your entrepreneurial aptitude, you can unlock career rewards that are virtually unheard of for employees.

Part I: PR Client Services

For someone who has learned how to do everything it takes to help a company mount and manage the PR aspects of an integrated marketing campaign at any scale – or how to use social media strategically and consistently to deliver Returns on Investments that score highly among the coveted Key Performance Indicators – by what means can they learn how to win and manage an account? By and large, that type of knowledge has previously required earning tenure within a PR firm. For you, this seasoned pro is putting those hard-earned secrets on the table.

From there, everything that follows on from securing an account is similarly divulged, analyzed, and worked-up for optimization. In your role, the core identity of a company is not only essential, but it also is subject to being improved upon, to elevate its potency and efficacy for stakeholders and customers alike. With the groundbreaking insights of proven experts, your abilities to fine-tune positioning, communications strategy, and tactics will rise to support the highest level of corporate ambitions.

Having illuminated and explored the entire landscape of corporate communications, the powers of this position are supercharged with inside knowledge of advanced account management, including exposure to the trade secrets of media relations expertise that are revelatory for aspiring PR professionals.

Finally, using decades' worth of experience, four elemental management philosophies are identified, compared, and contrasted. Sorting out the staples of promotional marketing according to probable fit, an innovative scheme is devised for shrewdly prescribing them to serve your clients' needs.

Part II: Agency Business

The arc of my agency primarily began with working inside a high-octane PR firm, then led to setting out on my own with a first account. Like some of my friends who largely operate "gig to gig" in service of whomever hires them, it is not always necessary to spend much time or effort building out one's business brand. Nonetheless, in my experience, the benefits of entrepreneurship multiply when we use our capabilities to bolster our own ventures, and by expanding and amplifying our expertise.

In this section, we will sound out your vision against the bedrock tenets of business success. Matched against the most important practices of an agency's operation, this example-rich, analytical discussion showcases the vast potential upside of self-service. Knowing it can be difficult to give such activities the attention they deserve, this case is made: Embracing them can change your world.

Undoubtedly, sharpening and deepening one's professional knowledge and skills elevates every aim we have identified; and yet, these extra efforts are also easy to backburner. This chapter uncovers sublime ways to build affinity around interests and client pursuits for maximum returns.

4 Introduction

Rounding out this motivational exploration of the big-picture aspects of business operation that set stellar enterprises apart, and which can be so difficult to sustain, this section culminates in an intelligent guide to scaling – and potentially selling – yours.

Part III: PR Master Toolset

On any given day, whatever the world's PR professionals are getting up to for their respective clients is likely to be minutely focused. At my desk, most activity can be tactical … perhaps researching, preparing, or pitching a new story, refining a media list, and/or tracking and reporting campaign results. Arguably the most valuable and impactful discipline has to do with planning.

Building atop this mountain of knowledge, this exploration of marketing and action plans gets ultra-specific. Using these and other sophisticated tools positions you to precisely, strategically triangulate client needs according to key objectives. From there, a hands-on tour through the world of presentations completes your training and challenges you to embrace the first of many career-defining assignments to come.

Prepare to Embark

My primary objective with this book is teaching you what I have learned. As you have already seen, I will be sharing many first-hand life experiences to activate your internal problem solver and help render lessons and key points. By studying what I have faced and achieved in this field, you can fully comprehend the rewards and pitfalls, and blaze a unique, highly rewarding career path. The resulting capabilities can transform your existence and give you the life of your dreams.

Please also give extra special attention to the exercises concluding each chapter. To seize the greatest rewards, give each Exploration section great care and attention: This is where your journey advances.

Exploration

1. Complete this sentence and fill in the author's name (if it does not sound familiar, Google it). "Starting your own business isn't just a job, _____ _____ _____ _____ _____." Who is the author (and are you sure about that)?

2. Do you believe a PR degree is necessary to succeed in business as a communications consultant? Why or why not?
3. Name five people who have dream jobs, from your point of view.
4. How much money are you worth per hour, when you are doing your absolute best work – and why are you worth that much?
5. In your opinion, what is the biggest perk of being a consultant, and the biggest downside?
6. In your opinion, what is the biggest perk of being an employee, and the biggest downside?
7. Using seven words or less, write a new slogan for an advertising campaign for a consultant.
8. Find and watch a TED Talk that has to do with communications strategy.
9. What event in history would you like to be able to attend, and why?
10. What could you talk about in a TED Talk of your own – either now or in several years when your career has taken off?

ii
My Story

It is a great honor for me to lead you on this voyage of specialized business education, based on a career trajectory that has been extremely fun and rewarding. Not so long ago, I was starting out, and since then, I have learned that every person and opportunity met along the way can absolutely transform the world. Since we are still strangers, here is a quick tour of some of the experiences illuminated in this book to help light the way for you.

As a high school student, I had earned good grades and demonstrated enough aptitude that college seemed like a sure thing. I gambled on winning a four-year Air Force Reserve Officer Training Corps scholarship that did not materialize and found myself entering the work force with no clear pathway forward. Still, the Air Force's powerful campaign urging everyone to "Aim High" pulled me in; as a Reservist, I got the leg up I needed to begin studying at the University of Central Florida.

By the time I graduated from UCF, I was intent on using the positive feedback I had earned as a writer to make my mark in the world of motion pictures. Two amazing openings occurred right away. First, as a VIP tour guide for the grand opening of Universal Studios Florida (USF), I was briefly allowed to step into the realm of Hollywood moguls and celebrities. I also earned a part-time job writing press releases for the impressive post-production business Century III, which made its home at USF.

Despite landing some potential game-changing developments in filmmaking and screenwriting, the results of my post-college efforts to land a starring role in "the industry" fell short. So, I applied myself freelancing – including word-processing work for defense contractors – and eventually, using the writing and photojournalist skills I had sharpened through my Air Force Reserve training, I started placing some nonfiction articles in trade publications. I also submitted a lot of creative writing to prominent literary reviews,

DOI: 10.4324/9781003177913-2

scoring a few placements and starting to understand what it meant to succeed as a professional writer.

With experience and determination, better prospects began arising. While the video scripts I wrote for major clients paid the bills, it was my technical writing skills – and my interest in film – that opened the most exciting doors. Between 1994 and 1997, I found work as a network TV script coordinator for HBO and others. That momentum led my wife and me to relocate to Los Angeles.

Even with lots of connections at the top of both the feature film and TV industries, success in screenwriting still eluded me. Still, 24 months of employment in LA gave my career a solid boost. It was the Century III experience, and my success writing articles for industry trade publications, that helped me land my first job on the West Coast. From there, I was the director of marketing for a creative production company in the promo space, which led to a career-opening position as an account executive for high-tech PR firm The Terpin Group (TTG).

At that point, I was no longer pining away for a career in the movies, for a few key reasons. First, I had learned that the production industry demands most of one's time – 14-hour days and six-day work weeks are standard. Being part of the crew on episodic TV series taught me a lot about my work preferences. At TTG, I earned good money working regular hours … but I also saw the difference between what the agency billed and what I was paid. So, after learning all the PR agency ropes over the span of about seven months, I was able to launch The Darnell Works Agency (DWA) and immediately double my income, while working from home.

This was an amazing turn of events for me. Once again, it became extra meaningful due to my focus on film and TV, and the people in my life at that time. One of my colleagues at TTG recommended me for an account she had previously handled. This became my first account in the commercial advertising industry. The client group was extraordinary, and it was essential in demonstrating my capabilities at the highest level. In other words, it was a perfect fit, and it set me on the path of independent success.

Within a year of launching DWA, my wife and I made another big move, leaving LA for the mountains of North Carolina and starting a family. At the time of our departure, my business was thriving. What would be the impact of leaving that dream factory for a small college town in the Appalachian Mountains? In short, we have come through several massive economic downturns, the unmeasurable upheaval of 9/11, and a global pandemic, in excellent shape.

At the beginning of my career journey, finding work was not easy, nor was it often fun or rewarding. It was certain to require me going to work at some location, doing my job according to a schedule set by my boss, and hoping that things would go well, that I would have some job security, and maybe some perks, eventually. The dreams of working from home, living in my choice location, earning over U.S. $100 per hour, and being able to pick and choose clients were beyond my reach. How in the world could I ever make them a reality?

This book is here to explain how I was able to achieve all these seemingly far-fetched aspirations. If you have similar career aims, read on. With diligence, we are going to elevate your journey.

As I am writing this and savoring the latest experiences, including everything I have learned to help you design and construct your Master Plan, I am keenly aware of a new level of achievement. The success of my business is now allowing me to dig back into those earlier career aspirations that were more personal, which I have previously been unable to prioritize due to needing to hustle to secure my and my family's financial needs. This book is one measure of the type of reward that can come from following my lead. For the first time in many years, screenwriting is also back on my agenda.

For me, the lesson seems to be this: Do great work for others and commit to it 100%. When things align and you have the security you desire, by systematically expanding your focus to address your own objectives, dreams can come true. It will take time and disciplined focus, no doubt… but thankfully, this journey is extremely rewarding.

Part I
PR Client Services

Topics Covered

Winning and Managing PR Accounts   11
Client Positioning and Communications Strategy   30
Investors and Investor Relations   39
Advanced PR Account Management   49
Advanced Communications and Marketing Strategies and Tactics   73

1
Winning and Managing PR Accounts

As we begin this new journey together, you already have some knowledge of the educational and life experiences which led to me becoming an account executive at the successful public relations firm The Terpin Group (TTG). That career-changing development took place in 1999, when TTG had offices in Los Angeles, San Francisco, and New York. In this book's introduction, I also mentioned some of the business intricacies I have homed in on – including philosophical and practical discussions – to better understand how, when, where, and why the steady application of sound communications practices can radically alter careers and enterprises. If you have read The Communications Consultant's Foundation, you possess an excellent working knowledge of vital concepts including brands, branding, creativity, leadership, strategy, objectives, integrated marketing, business development, profitability, and project management. The question is, can you convince another business owner that you are the perfect candidate to help them add professional communications capabilities to their operation, and then fill that tall order?

Yes, you can, if you have been actively participating in incorporating what I have shared, building your brand, embracing the challenges presented and preparing yourself to be a proactive, strategic communicator dedicated to exceeding your clients' expectations. Winning the first account is likely to be the hardest, but if all goes well, that achievement will ignite a chain reaction. Let's take a moment to fully assess the phenomenal foundation you now stand upon.

1. You are a proactive communications leader dedicated to the success of yourself and others, guided by one or more codes of ethics.
2. You embrace the importance of creativity, problem solving – and innovative approaches to problem finding.

DOI: 10.4324/9781003177913-4

3. You are committed to ongoing learning, and to strategic planning on a regular basis.
4. You are always ready to position yourself as the ideal candidate according to your core strengths, and to demonstrate your expertise.
5. You have a solid brand identity and open communications channels, and you can guide others in thoughtfully developing their own personal and business brands, and their strategic promotional campaigns.
6. You are the proprietor of your own business consultancy, and you have a Leadership Brand that fits your objectives.[1]
7. You are increasing your strengths in all facets of the key skill set for a communications consultant.
8. You can explain how you can make a strategically sound impact on a client's business objectives over time – and intelligently use media assets to maximize impact in its storytelling initiatives.
9. You have one or more case study to demonstrate your expertise in action.
10. Your understanding of the continuous customer journey, business development, strategy, and other essentials of business – including project management – positions you to focus on the right tactics to serve your clients' business objectives strategically, starting immediately.

The Initial Interview

Moving forward based on our common understanding of business development, customer service, and integrated marketing in action, attracting and retaining customers is a nuanced science unto itself. I have found success in navigating this vast terrain by focusing on objectives – mine and those of my clients. If they are calling you, someone at that company has identified a need that has been deemed important, and most likely, there is strong interest in addressing it starting very soon. Your goal, then, is to listen well enough to fully understand the nature of that need. From there, the challenge is to convince the caller that you are the best person to guide them forward, and to establish an agreement that will make you a leader in addressing their needs.

Whether the initial interview happens in person or by phone, this interaction is a test to determine your worthiness for an assignment. The simple way of looking at this is your potential client has some needs, and they want to explain those to you and then determine if they feel confident in your ability to address them to their satisfaction. Whenever the phone rings or an email query arrives, my response is usually to the point: (1) Thank you very much for thinking of me; (2) let's set up a call to discuss this in more detail; and (3) let's exchange emails and set a date and time for the call.

Before the interview takes place, I find the time to connect with those who have reached out on LinkedIn, and I go through their website, subscribe to their newsletter if that is an option, examine and connect on their social media channels, and perhaps do some research to analyze what media coverage they have generated. For the call itself, I use a set of questions I refer to as a Needs Analysis. It is especially important to listen and take notes, to capture whatever information comes to light in the interview.

If you pass this initial test and are invited to submit a proposal, its first section is where you will need to create a short Situation Analysis accurately portraying the client company's status and its reasons for seeking professional PR help. Also, remember this: Although this is an interview of you by another company's executives, it also represents your best chance to determine whether they are going to be a good fit for you before you become obligated to serve them.

Normally, the company's lead for setting up the interview will begin by presenting a quick overview, which will provide an explanation of why they are considering adding PR. Here are the questions you can expect them to have for you, along with some suggested answers from my playbook.

1. Q: How do you work, what is the process?

    I would like to run through some questions together, which will give you a good sense of how my process works. How does that sound?

2. Q: What are your rates, how are we billed?

    You may have seen on my website – my minimum retainer is U.S. $3,500 per month, and that is based on an hourly rate, which is currently U.S. $215 per hour (that translates into about an hour per weekday, on average). I use a standard letter agreement that is very client-friendly – after the first month, either party can wrap things up within 10 days by providing notice, and after the initial term, it continues on a month-to-month basis. If you choose to go in a different direction, I want you to be able to do that. This agreement is the same one I have in place with all my clients, and it has served us all very well.

3. Q: How do you feel about our chances for generating media exposure?

    There is a spectrum of media outlets, with hard or breaking news outlets on one side and trade-media outlets on the other. By taking a balanced approach in engaging with trade media outlets and also professionally pitching breaking news outlets when we have relevant stories for them, I feel we will be able to make great progress on your objectives. I will aim to do excellent work on your behalf.

4. Q: What are the next or the first steps?

Within a week after this call, I will send you a proposal, which provides a menu of the services I can offer, subject to your needs. I will also send a simple letter agreement. Once you have signed the agreement and arranged payment, we will begin with a deeper dive into your positioning, assess your communications channels, and ensure we have the most strategically sound messaging in place everywhere. I will then research and build our media database and begin organizing our communications initiatives.

Here are the questions I present to potential clients from my Needs Analysis. Rarely do I ask them all, because many of them may be answered in the client's initial comments, or I may decide to research certain answers on my own.

1. How's business?
2. What led you to consider expanding your PR efforts?
3. What does your company specialize in?
4. Who is your main competition?
5. What is most unique about your company?
6. What are your main marketing objectives?
7. What are the most important aspects of your marketing plan that I should be aware of?
8. What news-worthy projects or announcements are coming up?
9. What media outlets are of the most interest to you?
10. What else is coming up soon that is important for the company? Involvement in industry events, speaking engagements, etc.?
11. How important are awards programs, and are you interested in having me monitor those and/or coordinate submissions?
12. When does the PR campaign need to begin?

Having asked these questions and gathered notes on the answers, you are now in great position to create a proposal. What remains to be done is positioning yourself as the perfect candidate for their needs and demonstrating your expertise. The talking points I use for those purposes begin with three triangles.

- The McNeill PR Triangle: This framework was shared with me by Digital Kitchen's co-founder and CEO Don McNeill in an initial interview for his company's PR account. According to Mr. McNeill, PR came down to three things: (1) the work; (2) a company's efforts to communicate with its PR partner; and (3) the capabilities of that PR partner.

If you introduce this framework by saying that a successful business leader has asserted that PR campaigns have those three main ingredients, be sure to emphasize that the first two components are in the hands of the client company. Therefore, the results you generate will be built on the quality of their work and the support they will provide to you.

- <u>Lead, follow, or get out of the way:</u> I often tell my clients that we cannot do PR on something until they have a happy client ... and sometimes, making the client happy is impossible. There are also other reasons why every company development is going to need to be assessed individually to determine whether it is a fit for being promoted. Assuming it is a go, we then need to determine if we are going to lead, follow, or get out of the way.

This filter is based on the knowledge that clients often have clients, and in that chain of command, there may be other PR professionals engaged to lead the PR strategy around a given project. When others are "leading" the efforts, the best you can hope for is to be granted permission to "follow" with your client's effort, after the leaders' plans go into effect. In the absence of another leader, that is a momentous opportunity for your client to leverage your capabilities and offer to extend your services to its client. To make this clearer, imagine your client is a toy maker, and an inventor comes to them to make a special commission. If the inventor has no PR team, your client can offer your services to lead the PR campaign, where your objectives focus on getting people to stock or purchase the toy, versus just promoting your client's brand, strengths, and stories. In this situation, it is important to remember who is paying the bill and to ensure they approve of all your efforts.

The final alternative – "get out of the way" – is what happens when your client is not able to secure permission to lead or follow. Normally, there are still opportunities there, like promoting whatever news coverage does come out on social media, adding the project to your client's website, and possibly submitting the project for awards, if those steps are permissible.

- <u>Big, medium, and/or small:</u> Based on whether we are leading, following or otherwise, and how the company feels about a given project, together we will then determine the scale of our promotional effort(s). "Big" would be a press release, perhaps with the goal of attempting to place an exclusive or angling to generate wide media coverage. "Medium" might just be some limited pitching to place a story or two, and "small" would be website and social media seeding.

By now, you can hopefully see how explaining these three triangles positions you as being a person who knows how to strategically evaluate PR opportunities and then move into certain plans of action, based on situational analyses. In the initial call, you could potentially stop there, ask your clients what other questions they have for you, provide those answers, and let them know when they can expect to receive your proposal.

The importance of being extremely familiar with the contents of your proposal cannot be overstated here; you will need to be prepared to use it to answer questions, and to let your potential clients know what to expect when they receive it. If you have the time and want to demonstrate your expertise even further, you might explain these standard components of a PR program you will be aiming to develop and use on your client's behalf.

- Objectives: Depending upon the priorities, your efforts might focus more on legal, HR, customer service, marketing, and/or sales, for a few examples.
- Boilerplate and positioning: Early efforts will emphasize the standardization of these vital aspects of their business communications.
- Executive bios will be organized and/or written, especially for the company's leaders.
- News Releases: When project-driven, these are subject to client approvals.
- Preparing to pitch, including analyzing media targets of interest and gathering contact information.
- Assessing, advising on and/or managing social media channels, depending upon client needs.
- Exploring original or company-driven projects and initiatives which can make a company more interesting (e.g., REI's #OptOutside policy and promotional campaigns, and the Box Tops for Education program operated by General Mills).
- Researching speaking opportunities, developing speaking topic proposals, and pitching, if those activities are of interest. If so, bear in mind that pursuing speaking engagements can be very time-intensive, and that success often requires a dedicated, sustained effort.

Having answered their questions and explained how you will approach the handling of their communications needs, hopefully you will have passed the initial test, and they will be eager to receive your proposal. Assuming you are encouraged to continue the pursuit, you now have some writing to do.

The Proposal: Gearing Up

Take comfort in this: The language you present in your proposal provides the architecture that will support everything you might do for your client, no matter how long the relationship lasts. You and I both stand on the shoulders of giants in this regard. My gratitude begins with Michael Terpin and extends to all those who contributed to the proposal language I inherited in pursuing new accounts through TTG.

Venturing out on my own and closely examining the information I felt I needed to share with my potential clients to close deals, I made a lot of tweaks to the TTG proposal template of 1999. There were some practical reasons for this, as I am sure you can understand; if you do not feel comfortable proposing to confidently provide some service for a business, that is a good reason to rewrite your proposal language to clarify your confidence level, for one example. Presenting a proposal for The Darnell Works Agency and its sole proprietor necessarily had to differ from a TTG one, with its hierarchy of available account professionals. Further, I felt that if I could simply say what needed to be said to secure an agreement, and then get to work demonstrating my value and fulfilling my clients' expectations, the proposal would have done its job. To accommodate these emphases, I removed anything I felt was non-essential. That left a few important matters from TTG's language to be addressed by other means.

For educational purposes, I want to examine vital language that appeared in the 1999 TTG proposal more closely. Well worth mentioning that document formed the basis for the U.S. $20,000 per month account I helped win during my first week with the firm, and its core language underwrote millions of dollars' worth of agency business over the course of more than a decade. This model proposal provided a tried-and-true formulaic engagement approach, leading with an analysis highlighting the particulars of the client company's current situation. Next came an overview touting TTG's strengths, then a more in-depth walkthrough of TTG's work approaches and bios for its executives, followed by a detailed breakdown of the elements of the communications program being proposed, to include costs … and on page 13, a parting summary. It was always used in conjunction with a letter agreement clients needed only to sign and deliver, along with a check for the first month's retainer, to put the relationship into effect. Appendix includes an example of a 2021 DWA proposal and letter agreement used to form and structure one of my business relationships.

Regarding my need to customize my toolset for establishing my own client relationships, once again, my goals have been to reduce proposal and letter agreement language to the essentials, and whenever possible, to make the terms more client friendly. As mentioned, this has been necessary to adapt documents that were presenting a team of professionals dedicated to "leaving no publicity opportunity untouched" at a monthly rate representing half a year's worth of PR budget for a typical DWA client. The scale of effort expected for companies paying U.S. $8,000 per month in 1999 – the lowest retainer I saw accepted at TTG during my tenure there – is going to have fundamental differences from those paying U.S. $3,500 for a one-person communications consultancy. Naturally, the location of the PR partner represents another major factor in what many client companies are willing to pay for; having professional representation in LA, San Francisco and NYC carries a lot of weight. For all these reasons, my offerings and fees are more streamlined than the ambitious packages proposed by TTG two decades ago.

With these clarifications in mind, let's review something from TTG's 1999 proposal. Whereas that documentation referred to its hybrid client description as a unified public relations message, to me, that is my client's all-important positioning statement. Sorting that out effectively continues to be my primary focus throughout the life of a PR campaign. In my proposal, this is addressed in section three, "Key Message," which follows the Situation Analysis, and a short treatment called Approach, where I explain my qualifications for serving the client's needs. By my account, those qualifications build upon my accomplishments as "a Scripps-Howard Fellowship-winning journalist and writer," among others.

TTG's introductory proposal language quickly made the case for the "Dynamic Relationship" and "Professional Writing" – two sections I do not include, but which are important to understand and build upon. To explain, the work of a communications consultant relies on high quality information exchange to be effective. Committing to daily contact is essential for both parties in establishing a working relationship that can flourish, given the challenges that come with fulfilling expectations in the realm of PR. Is this something that needs to be expressed in a proposal, or can it simply be put into practice? Here is my answer: The word "daily" never appears in my proposal.

Professional writing is another point of emphasis I attempt to make evident through my work, versus calling it out in my proposal. Between the Situation Analysis and my Approach section, I aim to make it perfectly clear that I am qualified, and to use words that are engaging and convincing.

The Proposal Itself

Once again, from the top: We are seeking to perfect a document that will allow your potential clients to see what services you offer, where you begin by addressing it to them personally. There is a cover page with their logo and yours, then page one begins with the Situation Analysis. What is often a single paragraph in my proposals explains the particulars of the client's business at the point in time where the need for professional PR has put us in contact. A second paragraph makes the case for my expertise.

Section Two, Approach, fortifies my qualifications while also summarizing how I work in handling media relations, with a brief treatment on the need to be diligent, careful, and strategic. I mentioned how the TTG proposal framed up the discussion around the Key Message; appearing as my third section, I come at this somewhat differently. While I do adopt TTG's approach and explain how important it is, I do not include their current positioning language*. Instead, I present approximately ten boilerplates that I round up from companies on their competitive horizons. Sometimes, these boilerplates present companies from fields where the client only aspires to compete. This is an original aspect of my proposals which elegantly drives home important lessons about the power of key messages, while priming my potential client for the task of perfecting theirs.

> * Here, I will interject an insight crystallized for me by Blair Enns, CEO of Win Without Pitching, and author of The Win Without Pitching Manifesto and Pricing Creativity. Speaking on the topic of business development and using the analogy of how a doctor approaches a patient (examine, diagnose, treat, re-examine), Mr. Enns asked us if we would ever attempt to diagnose a patient without first performing a thorough examination. This scenario was raised to address the all-too-familiar situation where marketers are invited to pitch for clients without an in-depth understanding of the company they are seeking to serve. As a suggested policy, Mr. Enns advised only beginning to fix client problems <u>after</u> one is hired. I have attempted to reflect that sage advice in my proposal presentation on the Key Message.

Section Four, Strategic Objectives, owes much to TTG's proposal language. Eight descriptive statements set out a comprehensive framework designed to deliver anything and everything the client has in mind to achieve in engaging with a dedicated PR professional. The next section on Target Media is comprised of a short paragraph in my version, in contrast to the half-page of detailed diligence in TTG's U.S. $20,000-per-month version. In theirs, the various types of media outlets are defined, and specific examples of the media to be targeted in the campaign are listed. In a DWA proposal, Mr. Enn's directive is further served, as I summarize the full range of media outlets I have reached in the past for my clients and indicate that similar diligence will be applied to generating exposure on behalf of the new client, in support of its specific promotional objectives.

Section Five, Ongoing Monthly Services, is a half-page section using a streamlined version of TTG's model. The more ambitious approach filled more than three pages with detailed descriptions of specialized services – including the handling of large-scale media events – which certainly factored into TTG's ability to win such accounts on its terms. Although I am confident in being able to handle many aspects of event development and marketing, the fact that it is not my forte is one reason my proposals do not address the development of events. Still, by offering to provide the following services according to the client's priorities and budget, I have found success, and I feel you can, too.

- Market Positioning
- Corporate Image-Building Campaign
- News Bureau
- One-on-One Interviews
- Awards Competitions
- Speaking Engagements
- Networking and Business Development Opportunity Research and Exploration

From that point forward, a single page provides more than enough canvas to clarify the Costs (with reference to my letter agreement), confirm my Availability, and provide a brief closing Summary.

The Letter Agreement and the Engagement

In the same way that the proposal follows the initial interview and formalizes its discussion into a cumulative framework that will organize the client/

agency relationship, the letter agreement aims to render a mutually acceptable contract that is enforceable by both parties. Over the span of about three pages, this agreement confirms what has been discussed, stipulates payment terms and consequences for non-payment, while also formally addressing other important matters of the relationship.

For those interested in the contract language I inherited from TTG which does not appear in my current agreement, there are two paragraphs I have removed. In the original, the period of the agreement stands for its full initial term (often 3 months at the minimum) and can only be terminated by the client for "Cause," defined as involving fraud or willful misconduct on the part of the agency. After that initial term, either party is at liberty to terminate the agreement with or without cause by giving the other party a minimum of 30 days' notice. In my experience, I have gotten to the place more than once where a situation arose with a client where I knew the best solution was to wrap things up quickly. Also, rather than having the longer period forced upon us all and introducing language about cause (with its negative connotations), I chose to simplify that section. The only mention of that word in my standard agreement (see Appendix) is to state that either party may terminate it with or without cause at any time after completion of the first month, by giving no less than 10 days' notice.

My other main revision from TTG's 1999 model contract removes a paragraph that warns the client against hiring staff members and puts a price on such an occurrence. While that is a legitimate concern for a larger agency, a sole proprietorship obviously has no need for that provision.

At the suggestion of my lawyer, an arbitration clause has been added into my letter agreement. As the final component of a series of activities designed to educate both the client and the agency about each other's needs and strengths, to clarify the work to be done together, and to forge a legal, binding relationship, I have found my version of the letter agreement to be essential and extremely effective. More than once, I have been asked to sign another company's contract, instead of them signing mine. A standard clause closed TTG's contract, stating that prior to signing the agreement, all parties were advised to seek legal counsel. Standing on that advice, I encourage you to follow this prescription and have a lawyer review any agreement you put forward or agree to, to ensure you fully understand your obligations. That way, if it becomes necessary to enforce the agreement, you will be as prepared as possible.

Thankfully, so far, I have never needed to have a lawyer involved to end an agreement on good terms. To me, returning money received on an account where a problem has arisen is always an option, but I have only had to take that step once, early in my career. In that situation, I knew my peace of mind was worth much more than the small fee I had received.

If all goes well, you will soon receive a signed letter agreement and a check for your first month's retainer. That impressive achievement will require you to begin earning your keep.

The Kick-Off

Whenever an organization makes a choice to formally engage with an outside consultant, it is a big deal. You can guarantee that someone there, if not every top-level executive, will be waiting for you to guide them on the next steps. If you were effective in your biggest jobs up to the point of winning the account (listening and assessing their situation), you should have a good handle on the essential facets that will frame up your communications plans. However, unless you have no choice but to jump right into the fray and work on getting that first story out into the world, it is often wise to usher your clients through a more formal and in-depth planning phase.

As suggested in the initial interview, even before the client signs your agreement, you can expect to be asked, "How do we get started? What are the next or first steps?" I've already shared a guideline for you, with this answer: "We will begin with a deeper dive into your positioning, assess your communications channels and ensure we have the most strategically sound messaging in place everywhere. I'll then research and build our media database and begin organizing our communications initiatives."

However, let's pause a moment. Now that you are engaged to help lead the PR efforts for this company, it is time for your strategic leadership to begin. If you feel it is most critical to better understand your client's operations and needs before swinging into action, this is the moment for you to make your case. After all, spending time to solicit answers to important questions is sure to clarify the objectives, thereby solidifying the strategies and tactics you and others will use to pursue the desired results and improving everyone's chances for success. Even so, having assessed your client's needs and established your ability to address them, the engagement should commence, with at least some consideration of the ground situation and what your instincts warrant.

- Are you directly engaging with the leader, or is your liaison coordinating with you and then having to report through the chain of command? This answer may prompt you to skew your early approach to the challenges your liaison is currently facing, versus larger issues affecting the company.

- Is this a well-managed organization that is patiently prepared to support your mission, or is PR further down the list of priorities? This answer may prompt you to skew your approach to demonstrate your capabilities sooner, versus doing more due diligence to better plan for longer term impact.
- Is something momentous transpiring which demands immediate attention? If so, you must rivet your attention to this development, knowing also that if you cannot assemble a strategically sound platform to support it, this relationship may quickly flounder.

Assessing such corporate, logistical, or management-oriented details of your new client's operations may alter your first steps with your client, since a crisis where your help is needed is sure to fully absorb your initial attention. Based on your best sense of your client's willingness to support campaign planning, choose whatever you feel will be your best approach, and lead the way.

To commence, here are some details I have included in the cover letter included in Appendix, where I propose a standard campaign start.

- If you have not already met the clients in person, it may be a good idea to offer to meet with them in their chosen location at some point during your first two months, at your own expense (discreetly clarifying that you will want to charge for the time that you spend meeting with them). This strategic idea is discussed in more detail in this chapter's upcoming section on Billing; if you choose to put it forward, proposing a date and location for this meeting will be a strong indication of your commitment to the relationship.
- Step One: Revisit positioning and ensure it is as strong as possible for the foreseeable future.
- Step Two: Identify key business objectives to be served through the PR campaign in the early going, and perhaps second-tier ones to be addressed down the road.
- Step Three: Inventory the company's branding and its owned media channels and discuss how those can be strengthened and used in unison to address its objectives.
- Step Four: Inventory "news-worthy" developments and plan how and when to use those – with the goal of establishing a content calendar for the immediate future or longer term.
- Step Five: Additional planning to support prioritized objectives – for example, media relations, awards, speaking engagements, recruiting, business development, and social media.

Formal Communications Planning

Again, depending upon the size and complexity of your new client's organization, proceeding through a formal communications audit may be an extremely valuable approach for everyone involved, especially you. Offering the unique ability to identify and survey both internal and external stakeholders in a company, being able to collect, analyze, and decipher the findings would put you in a pivotal position early into your relationship. Here are five articles you can use to help you formulate your approach in justifying, organizing, and completing a communications audit.

- "Five steps to conducting an effective communications audit" by Alejandro Licea: http://bit.ly/5caudit
- "Eight key steps for a successful communications audit" by Heather MacLean: http://bit.ly/4caudit
- "How to Conduct A Social Media Audit" by Kristy Morrison (Bolsinger): http://bit.ly/3caudit
- "Responsibilities of the PR Policymaker" by Deirdre Breakenridge: http://bit.ly/DBprPM
- "Communication Audits" by National School Public Relations Association: http://bit.ly/2caudit

The results of a communications audit can take many forms. Certainly, there will need to be a report that is sure to be of wide interest to the client company's executives. I engaged with PostWorks New York in May 2004. On June 22, I traveled to NYC to present my Strategic Marketing Plan to the company's chief executives. A fond take away from that meeting was the company's CEO holding up his copy and saying that everyone should treat it as our marketing bible moving forward. That highly productive DWA relationship continued for five years, serving PostWorks through to its acquisition.

The Communications Planning Fire Drill

Contrast that PostWorks scenario with one I ran into in October 2018. Contacted by a gentleman in San Francisco and invited to discuss PR for the high-profile leader of his client company, I was given access to a completed Strategic Communications Plan about an hour before our first conversation. I am sure you can see what a different opportunity this represents, versus having a group invite me to help them methodically formulate a communications program for their company, and then working together to activate it.

In the latter scenario, even before I was hired, I was essentially being asked to ingest their entire strategic communications plan and then tell them how to spring into action to address the objective they singled out.

There are many new business opportunities for communications consultants that fall in between these two examples, but it is a relatively safe bet that most of them are going to skew toward the fire drill. Even seasoned executives will expect validation of their expenditures relatively quickly, and who can blame them? The average lifespan for a Chief Marketing Officer at any given company is about four years[2]: Although you probably will not know whether your client's marketing leader is just settling in or on the way out, dynamics like this may make your job much more challenging. So, whether the planning has already been done for you or it quickly becomes clear that you must leap into solving some highly specific problem, the recipe I have shared is going to serve you well.

To register as effectively as possible, go through those five steps and work on preparing yourself for action according to what you learn. Chapters to follow will guide you through Positioning, Internal and External Communications alignment, and then, the vital aspects of being a communications consultant, including media relations.

Time and Record-Keeping

At TTG, we billed clients by the hour, working within our allotted monthly retainers to deliver results that kept our clients coming back. In 1999, here are the hourly rates included in our proposal materials.

- Agency President, $325 per hour; Chief Operating Officer, $225 per hour; Vice President/General Manager, $210 per hour; Group Director, $185 per hour; Account Manager, $165 per hour; Senior Account Executive, $140 per hour; Account Executive, $110 per hour; Assistant Account Executive, $90 per hour; Account Coordinator, $75 per hour; Intern, $40 per hour.

Charging by the hour is not the only – nor necessarily the best – basis for establishing a working relationship with your clients … but it is the one I have chosen, and it has served me very well. If you read Dr. Alan Weiss's book, "Getting Started in Consulting," you will encounter a full treatise extolling the virtues of flat and value-based fees, where hourly fees are allegedly unconscionable.[3]

Some of my colleagues in the business do operate on a flat-fee basis, and I feel there is more than one upside. Still, as an honest, hard-working professional who aims to keep life relatively simple, to find clients I enjoy working with who are committed to making PR part of their business and working with me if I can show them value, I embrace the security and peace of mind that my way of doing business affords me and my clients. The arguments Dr. Weiss makes are vehement, which makes sense, as he must defend his value-based approach and convince his readers it is the only way to go. If you follow his counsel, it seems your fees could increase exponentially, and as such, perhaps I leave some money on the table by billing hourly. Earning money at rates like those cited in TTG's 1999 proposal materials is plenty for me to aim for, and to make worthwhile for my clients.

In his book, Dr. Weiss asks if it favors us when clients must be prepared to pay for every instance of our service. My answer is yes. They know I am not a volunteer, and they also know that – like the taxi, Uber, or airplane they book to take them where they want to go – I am offering them a valuable service, where they already know the cost. Providing value at the agreed-upon rate, on the agreed-upon terms, is fair, square, and straightforward.

If you adopt this compensation model for your business, the question is, can you put a system in place to allow you to accurately track your time as part of your daily business operations? At DWA, I use time-tracking software built for this purpose, but I have found that even using a stopwatch, and sending emails to myself to track my activities, can do the job very effectively. A Google Sheets spreadsheet, or even a piece of paper, can be used to compile your time charges day by day. If you use QuickBooks for your business bookkeeping (highly recommended), you can use that to track your time. Also, there are apps like these which I have used that do an excellent job.

- Time Card for Android Free: http://bit.ly/tcaFREE
- Time Card for Android: http://bit.ly/tcANDrd

What I find equally important to the daily time entries are the descriptions that explain the day's activities for my clients' oversight. At the end of a given period, when I deliver the month's Activity Report and an invoice for the period to come, that is a momentous reckoning. It is perfectly reasonable to expect that the client's executives will review this receipt, that the activities it illuminates (based on your descriptions) will be judged alongside any other feats you have helped to accomplish, and if all adds up, your relationship will continue. Otherwise, presenting that report may be one of your final steps on behalf of that client.

Be sure to review the sample Activity Report I am including in Appendix to see how I carefully construct them, how I report the day-to-day activities, and how I total them. My aim is to over-deliver by 10% in terms of hourly billings compared with their retainer, and to add so much value that PR expenditures are perceived as slam-dunk investments.

Billing

Your website is one place you can explain your costs and terms of doing business to potential customers. Based on the hourly rate you feel you can justify, and the number of hours you feel will be necessary to demonstrate your value to your clients and address their needs from one month to the next (or, to complete their project, if you decide to bill on a project basis), communicating this fee to the world is well advised.

From there, the fact that you will bill for this fee is addressed in the letter agreement (again, if you are proceeding on a project basis and your client agrees to pay your fee, neither party may feel that a letter agreement is necessary), and upon receiving a signed letter agreement, your client will be expecting you to present an invoice.

At TTG, I learned that it is industry standard for PR professionals to be paid in advance, and payment for the first invoice I issue to a client is always either "due upon receipt" or within 15 days if I am feeling confident and generous. For ongoing accounts, per my letter agreement, I also provide an invoice 30 days in advance of the next period and let them know I hope to receive payment against it as close as possible to the next period's start date.

Your proposal also addresses expenses which you will be entitled to recover in certain circumstances. This language comes straight from the 1999 TTG proposal template: "Typical expenses include postage, photocopying, fulfillment, telephone, mileage, parking, delivery services, clipping services and press release distribution services. Out-of-town travel expenses include airfare, hotel, transportation, parking, and meals." TTG's 1999 contract addressed these matters further, obliging clients to pay a standard agency mark-up fee of 17.65% of the total expenses incurred on the client's behalf.

Note here that my proposal language adds a couple of lines: "If approved monthly expenses total less than U.S. $75, they will not be charged. There is no mark-up on expenses." Why? For a client company agreeing to pay my monthly retainer, I have seen that the time spent getting expenses approved, and then breaking them out and billing them, is something of a drag. Not charging a mark-up is a means of showing integrity and promoting trust. Also, having some expenses to present for tax purposes is beneficial for my agency.

Remember my suggestion to visit your client relatively soon after your partnership begins? Covering the cost for your own travel and your own hotel is gracious, it represents a valuable investment into the new relationship, and this practice has served me well. However, in all honesty, this "in-person visit" is not exactly standard for me, as my clients generally understand that for me to be effective at my job, I need to be in my own office. Also, if the time/expenses for this trip are formidable, I have often found it better to skip this offer and focus instead on getting to work (after all, there is always Zoom). If you adopt the suggestion to visit a client at your expense, again, make sure they understand that you are still intending to bill for your time during your meetings.

Regarding expenses, I will add the recommendation that instead of you incurring a cost and then having to file for reimbursement, it is better if you can arrange for your client to cover that cost directly. Whenever you can present the actual bill directly to your client for payment, or gain permission to have payment applied to your client's credit card, that will save you time and expense.

Finally, if a client decides to wrap up your account, you may find yourself needing to refund some unused portion of a monthly retainer and needing to cancel some invoice you have issued in advance. It is my experience that having these billing policies and procedures in place is a vast improvement over the one where you are awaiting payment. Any client that does not come through with payments when they are due is subject to violation of your letter agreement if you follow my lead. Hopefully, your clients will line up their payments with your requests, and this professional handling of these small but important matters will result in a regular stream of income, one client after another, and represent the life's blood of your communications consultancy.

Exploration

1. What are the main benefits of having your minimum terms of engagement expressed on your website?
2. Determine your hourly rate and the other terms of your minimum client engagement. How do you justify that hourly rate and minimum monthly retainer?
3. Prior to engaging with a potential client in an initial interview, line up at least two friends, colleagues, or family members to do a mock interview

with you, where they ask you the four standard questions. Answering those smoothly and confidently is a requirement for landing your first client.
4. In your mock interview, find your own way to introduce and talk-through (a) the McNeill PR Triangle, (b) lead, follow or get out of the way, and (c) the big, medium, or small framework.
5. Assuming a client invites you to provide a proposal and they sign your letter agreement, explain how you present them with a plan to get to work.
6. Describe the means you plan to use to ensure you are working on the right activities in the right ways to maximize your value for your client.
7. You may never be able to convince a client of the value of a communications audit if you have never completed one. So, pick a business entity, non-profit or institution where you have an in, and offer to do this work on a pro-bono basis (unless you can arrange a fee, in-kind barter arrangement or some other receipt). Track your time as you go, to learn how long it takes to complete such an undertaking. Upon completion, explain why you feel better prepared to impact the organization than if you had just been asked to support a smaller initiative where you were given standard communications guidelines.
8. For your own consultancy, use the five steps identified in the sample Cover Letter in Appendix to formulate a promotional campaign you can put into effect to set yourself apart, and execute that plan (tracking your time as you go, to learn how long all of this takes). Consider completing a more formal communications audit on your own behalf.
9. A potential new client wants to pay you many months' worth of retainer in advance, for tax purposes. Assess the pros and cons of this scenario and share your thoughts on how you would handle it.
10. Familiarize yourself with the idea of value-based compensation and formulate your rationale for being either hourly, flat-fee or value-based in how you handle business relationships. What is your rationale for your means of compensation?

Notes

1 Darnell, R. (2007, May 12). Leadership Brand-Building in One Easy Step. Universal Positive. https://up.darnellworks.com/?p=77
2 Kornferry. (2017, February 13). Age and Tenure in the C-Suite. Kornferry.com. http://bit.ly/C-Sage
3 Weiss, A. (2009). *Getting Started in Consulting* (3rd ed.). Wiley.

2
Client Positioning and Communications Strategy

To be perfectly honest, the preparation for writing this chapter was a much more in-depth learning experience than I imagined it would be. Essentially, I was reminded yet again of how lucky I have been to receive phenomenal instruction that has raised my capabilities in ways that have proven to be extremely valuable to my clients, and therefore, to me.

As an important part of my formative role at The Terpin Group (TTG), I guided many high-level clients in the development and use of their key messages. While I was already aware of the importance of positioning language prior to landing that job, those agency experiences taught me how crucial it is. Pitching a company and its stories to the world's most prominent journalists, the words used to set the venture apart either prove successful by earning the desired results, or otherwise.

Through my own firm, I have rewritten almost every one of my client companies' positioning statements, with consistent, positive results to show for our joint efforts. Let's scientifically validate the importance of solid positioning, review the experts' development guidelines, and highlight the benefits that come with success in this vital realm of business communications. Then, after exploring a means for assessing a company's drive to communicate proactively, we will examine the different types of internal and external initiatives that can lift enterprises to the highest levels.

Positioning

When a prospective customer meets a company's positioning and there is a fit, relationships can then advance. Think, for instance, of a simple sign stating, "The Doctor is in." For anyone needing a doctor who encounters it, what follows is easy to guess. You may already understand the importance of working with your clients to nail down the optimal unique, strategic description of their offerings, and uniting all parties around its use. As you will see, when approached systematically, the perfect positioning language almost writes itself. From there, it is highly likely to be instrumental in helping your clients accomplish their objectives.

Drawing upon every bedrock tenet of business success we have addressed, a shrewd positioning statement provides an elegant fulcrum. It is a resolution infused by mission, reputation, strategy, creativity, ethics, leadership, culture, innovation, fit, customer relationships, confidence, and storytelling. To focus in, consider these words from Blair Enns: "The goal of positioning is to reduce or eliminate competition."[1] That is a great start for substantiating this corporate communications focal point.

Remember also that the subtitle for the 2012 New Business Summit co-hosted by David C. Baker and Mr. Enns was, "Using Your Positioning for More Reward, Impact, Control, and Fun." Opening that conference, Mr. Baker extolled the virtues of firmly establishing one's expertise, emphasizing the resulting competitive advantages and the ability to command higher fees, for starters. Expertise is such an essential business topic for Mr. Baker that in 2017, he wrote a book about it entitled "The Business of Expertise." Through his considerable experiences helping creative agency principals position themselves, in part by bringing the same value to their clientele, he has proven that specialization is critical in differentiation.

To Baker and Enns, the benefits of strong positioning go beyond sales advantages and price premiums: "The more meaningfully different you are seen to be, the greater the impact that you can have on the buying cycle."[2] For those who look to these gentlemen as mentors, as I do, these insights are divine. In any service-based business, it is natural to feel that one's job consists of fulfilling whatever the client needs. This idea of having impact on the buying cycle is wonderfully tantalizing, helping us gain ground in the all-important balance of power, which makes or breaks business relationships.

In many ways, Mr. Enns' expertise was forged through his groundbreaking work helping design firms and advertising agencies learn to gain more power in the buy-sell relationship. While this mission led directly to a focus on positioning, he also discovered the need to explore and develop any client's product: the skills, capabilities, processes, and other unique assets that validate its expertise.[3]

Drawing further from Mr. Enns' article on why most creative firms do not scale, here is another pivotal insight.

- "Today, I see three variables to positioning that represent three steps: Positioning is strategy, articulated then proven. <u>Strategy</u> is essentially focus – the answer to the question, what business are you in? <u>Articulated</u> speaks to the consistent, differentiated claim that you make to the market. <u>Proven</u> speaks to the product you've amassed that allows you to back up your claim."

This formula guides the construction of a solid positioning statement, for use in a company's boilerplate (the "About" statement featured in standalone listings, and at the end of press releases). With help from Mr. Enns and G. Scott Shaw of Everclear Marketing, I crafted this boilerplate and positioning for The Darnell Works Agency.

- Now in its third decade of developing highly successful marketing, PR, and media strategies, <u>the Darnell Works Agency is the go-to PR firm for creative agencies, brands, and entertainment ventures</u>. Offering unmatched writing talent and inside media expertise, agency principal Roger Darnell sets his clients apart atop their industries. Already central to billions of positive media impressions worldwide, the agency's collaborations with leading business executives and media luminaries continue soaring to new heights.

As I have explained, in the proposal phase of client relations, I do enough research to present boilerplates like this from about ten of my new prospect's competitors. I then analyze these in comparison with what the prospect's principals have used up to that point, and what they have revealed about themselves regarding present status and objectives. From there, the process of devising the correct positioning is well explained on the website for Mr. Baker's The Business of Expertise book.[4]

- "Experts develop insight by isolating patterns in data; they convert those insights to wealth by crafting a unique positioning for which few available substitutes exist; and their confidence grows as the marketplace embraces their application of expertise."

Specifically regarding formulating positioning statements, Mr. Baker provides precise guidance in the 2Bobs podcast on Positioning Cheats: "The way I'd look at your positioning is discipline for market. So, what do you do and for whom do you do it? ... If you've got a lot of population density after proclaiming your discipline for market, then it's incumbent on you to add a really strong perspective, a polarizing perspective."

If you have done your homework well, after assessing the merits of a dozen boilerplates for companies operating in a similar niche of industry with the goal of helping your client find the right words to set their expertise apart in meaningful ways, it should not be too hard for you to write a fittingly unique description. With their guidance, the result will crystallize, and that key message and its attendant language will perfectly illuminate the company's vital essence. It will be tested every day; it will probably need to change sooner or later; and, when it works, marketplace rewards will abound.

In 2018, I landed a remarkable new client named Bob Bonniol. His business MODE Studios had been around for more than 15 years by that time, but at the end of 2017, the company was on the verge of unveiling some amazing achievements. A lot of language was already being used on its internal and external marketing channels, and I was excited about both the opportunity to fortify its positioning and the rewards to come from those efforts. Through my research, I saw that two major MODE competitors, which are sometimes project partners, used the positioning of "experiential marketing agency" and "brand experience agency," respectively. I proposed this: "Hybrid experience agency MODE Studios creates transformative moments that engage and inspire."

To say the least, it was well received, and adopted immediately with no reservations. Relatively early into that year, it went live everywhere. That March, when Mr. Bonniol was invited to give a talk to the staff of another collaborative business partner, the session was live-streamed. It was there I learned that Mr. Bonniol was still coming to grips with the positioning. When he explained to the group that his PR firm had told him that his company is now a "hybrid experience agency," the words were delivered like the punch line of a joke. From what I could see on camera, there was no laughter ... though I did get the sense that the audience was hooked and ready to hear whatever he had to say next. The doctor was in, and he had the undivided attention of every patient within earshot. Over the course of that year, the marketplace embraced MODE Studios in every conceivable way, and our positioning efforts continue providing a solid foundation.

Worth mentioning here is the famed <u>elevator pitch</u>. The idea behind this much-discussed phenomenon is, if you meet someone important in an elevator, you have the amount of time it takes before the doors re-open to explain your business to them (or whatever you hope to interest them in, whether it is your screenplay, your vacation rental, or your Corvette). Sticking with the business application, this concept has wide adoption in Silicon Valley, and Entrepreneur Magazine has built an original series around it: https://entrepreneur.com/watch/elevatorpitch. To see the importance of a key message in presenting a business venture, I encourage you to invest some of your time watching Entrepreneur's fascinating show – particularly the moments when the contestants' pitches begin.

If you happen to find yourself in an elevator with any VIPs, and you can present yourself, it is highly advised to use your well-crafted positioning statement to introduce your business. My version sounds like this: "My name is Roger Darnell, I'm the principal of The Darnell Works Agency, the go-to PR firm for creative agencies, brands and entertainment ventures." When interests overlap, the standard response is, "We should talk."

The Drive for Superiority

To extend our thinking on these subjects, let's return once more to Mr. Enns' article addressing the scaling of creative firms. That writing's introduction brings readers to understand this: Mr. Enns' greatest impacts from sustained use of his talents have come from helping his clients change how they do their work, then codifying their efforts through the development of proprietary strategy models. To comprehend the article's full meaning, I highly recommend you to take it all in. I am extending this connection for multiple reasons; first and foremost, let's acknowledge that various levels of performance apply to every endeavor. For those who approach business scientifically, matching the highest performance levels offers the greatest likelihood for achieving superior results.

What do you consider to be the right way to go about your work, and how much emphasis is placed on procedural consistency within your client organizations? To Mr. Enns, codifying strategy models to establish a company's unique approaches toward diagnosing its clients' problems and fixing them is a proven means for fulfilling his core value proposition – as an expert on new business development for agencies. He even advocates for most client companies to dedicate internal strategists to help develop proprietary strategic models that can be used to build the type of corporate growth that is sustainable. To me, this represents the top-tier level of communications proficiency. As a prescription for business success, its effectiveness is well established.

Internal Communications Spectrum

Another source supporting further investment into what is essentially a company's internal communications discipline comes from the body of knowledge surrounding the Greiner Curve.[5] According to Mr. Greiner's studies, over time, companies seeking to grow typically experience six specific problems, each representing its own stage and requiring certain challenges to be overcome. To progress to the next higher phase, additional investments must be made. For instance, advancement to the fourth stage involves procedural standardization to support growth (Figure 1).

Sounds familiar, right? Following this logic, it makes sense that within some organizations, fulfilling your communications mission will involve supporting a sophisticated set of objectives, which are rigorously dedicated to the documentation of the company's operations, for purposes of internal learning, refinement, and preparation for growth. Let's designate these extra ambitious business ventures as Alphas.

In the circumstance where you are serving an Alpha, certain internal items are likely to be given priority in the communications suite. Consider any enterprise where the theme of "design thinking" gets attention: In such settings, communications opportunities are likely to abound for research, assessment, reporting, and analysis ... marking such ventures as having high potential for

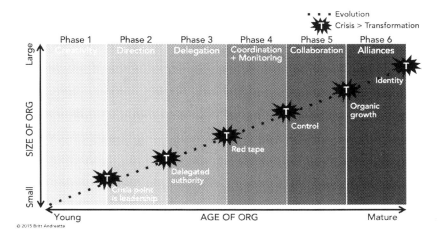

Figure 1: Phases of Org Growth[6]

Source: Andreatta, Britt: "Nurture and Anticipate Growth with the Greiner Curve," brittandreatta.com, Sep. 8, 2018: http://bit.ly/2wUT5yC

fit. Plotting any company's level on the Greiner Curve is yet another means for appraising its propensities toward professional communications.

For companies that are not overtly dedicated to systematically optimizing their operations, a focus on internal communications initiatives like the following is often rare.

Table 1: Internal Communications Initiatives

Job Applications	Policy and Procedures Manuals	Memoranda
Organizational charts	Internal email	Intranet
Training materials	Performance appraisals/reviews	Employment/exit interviews
Corporate presentations	Newsletters	Strategic/marketing plans

For a company seeking to grow and maximize its opportunities for success, a strong case can be made for standardizing all areas of corporate communications. Recognizing a company's inclinations, whether it is an Alpha or otherwise, can help you aim accordingly in scaling its communications needs, and in determining how far you feel it can go over time.

External Communications Spectrum

While there is much evidence to encourage entrepreneurs to address their internal communications standards prior to opening their doors to commerce, many businesses are more inclined to follow a "lemonade stand" approach. Metaphorically speaking, with a few lemons, water, sugar, a pitcher, some cups, a table, and a sign, the operation hastily opens in its parents' front yard with the hope of attracting business. That strong desire to focus first on one or more sales transactions is supported by a "learn-as-we-go" mindset toward most other aspects of management. In my experience working in the creative industry, it is surprising how many businesses fit this model, going project to project, doing what is necessary in that gig economy to make ends meet, and giving zero attention to anything resembling a codified strategy model.

I explain this as a means of clarifying my business perspective on all of this, which is rooted in service. If my clients are purely focusing on the next gig through their businesses, then my best bet at meeting their expectations is to increase their abilities to win that gig. Still, all this expert knowledge illuminating the inner workings of Alphas is here for us all to leverage as opportunities arise. Grounded in scientifically proven strategic business approaches, we are uniquely positioned to exceed our clients' expectations.

Take stock of the following examples of standard external communications initiatives, which are likely to appear on your client's PR agenda and require your attention. For each one, think about the extra values that can multiply the benefits, when they reflect solid positioning and all the other strategic and tactical firepower you bring to bear, based on your expanding education.

Table 2: External Communications Initiatives

Website	Marketing Communications	Sales Communications
Customer service communications	Recruiting communications	Investor relations communications
Social media communications	PR/media relations	Thought leadership
Speeches	Seminars/webinars	Newsletters

In summary, the described Alpha company represents the best example of a winning internal communications strategy. When it comes to external communications, the ideal is alignment across all channels, where the company's mission, its key messaging, its values, and its authentic truths appear, with up-to-date evidence of why and how the company matters to its target audiences.

Exploration

1. Why is it important to eliminate competition, and how does a positioning statement help with that?
2. If as a businessperson you can position yourself to impact the buying cycle with potential clients, what are the main advantages? List three.
3. Would you rather be a generalist or an expert? Validate your choice in the context of your business objectives.
4. You have been told a lot about the framework for an effective positioning statement, which is essentially a unique, strategic description, typically found within a company's boilerplate. Research and compile ten boilerplates for communications consultancies, with at least three of them being located within your region, making note of their positioning statements.

5. Write a positioning statement for yourself as a consultant and flesh it out into a boilerplate for your consultancy. Share that with at least three respected colleagues and rewrite as necessary.
6. Think about your own internal communications strategy. Where does your business fall on the Greiner Curve? Formulate your plans for handling your internal communications over time. For the three regional communications consultancies identified in your answer to question 4, see if you can assess their external communications strategy and establish some objectives based on their perceived successes or shortcomings.
7. In evaluating your external communications strategy, spend the time to ensure that your latest positioning language appears in your owned media channels and on social media. Does this "brand campaign" deserve more of a campaign push? If so, dive in.
8. Is there a "The Doctor is in" sign that might lead to new business opportunities for you, or someone you know who is struggling in business? Describe all relevant details of your idea.
9. Knowing what you know, if you were asked to open a lemonade stand within ten miles of your home, where would you put it? Next, if you had U.S. $5000 to invest, what would you do to try to build your lemonade stand venture to maximize returns?
10. Intelligently positioning a company is essential for media relations, and this becomes obvious when pitching a journalist on behalf of a company. Describe three stories that a newspaper reporter might write, and author a short pitch aimed at getting your imaginary client into each of those stories.

Notes

1 Enns, B. (2019, June 12). The Armor-Piercing Introduction. Win Without Pitching. http://bit.ly/wwpIntro
2 Baker, D., & Enns, B. (2018, February 21). Positioning Cheats. 2Bobs. http://bit.ly/2B-pc
3 Enns, B. (2019, June 12). Why Creative Firms Don't (Really) Scale. Win Without Pitching. http://bit.ly/wwpNoSc
4 Baker, D. (2017, August 1). The Business of Expertise. https://www.expertise.is
5 Petrone, P. (2016, December 2). Greiner Curve, 6 Stages Organizations Goes Through as They Mature. LinkedIn Learning Blog. http://bit.ly/Gcurve
6 Andreatta, B. (2021, February 17). Nurture and Anticipate Growth with the Greiner Curve. BrittAndreatta.com. http://bit.ly/2wUT5yC

3
Investors and Investor Relations

For my business, there have never been outside investors; this is true for most of the companies I have handled in my career as well, but not all of them. Nonetheless, these days, even the humblest startups or consultants imagine using other people's money to achieve success. Chances are, doing so would be a good – and possibly, a necessary – choice for at least some of them. While there are plenty of reasons to build companies without outside investors, from my research, sooner or later, any venture aiming to go public will probably need the security and other benefits that come from having negotiated large-scale outside investments. Investors are also vital to many businesses that remain private and have no intentions of ever going public.

What are the reasons for and against outside investors? Who invests in companies, why do they do it, what is Investor Relations (IR), and why is IR widely considered the highest level of PR mastery? To ensure you are aware of these top-tier business developments, let's explore some rationales for business lending, and the best resources for your education in the realm of venture finance. Together, we will also examine some of the tenets and practices of IR, so you can leverage them in your efforts for any company you serve.

Skip Investors, or Seek Them?

Beginning first in the setting of the private communications consultancy, I believe in certain approaches at the ground level. For starters, if you can take one dollar and make it multiply, you have a money-making proposition (and if you do not, you may be better off to just keep thinking). By exploring that proposition mindfully, you can innovate as you see fit, and attempt to increase profitability, if that is of interest. Perhaps profits will increase, but if they don't and you wind up losing everything including your original dollar,

DOI: 10.4324/9781003177913-6

at least you did so without owing anything to anyone else, right? This simple scenario is the one I have used to successfully operate my business in a way that appeals to me. Whatever I do, I am free to carry out in my chosen way ... and end up owning everything, owing nothing to investors.

Writing for Forbes, Startup Professionals Founder and CEO Martin Zwilling directly addresses my surprise at the high number of entrepreneurs who start courting investors almost immediately.[1] As presented in his writing and just about anywhere you research the subject of investors, pursuing outside investment is a full-time job on its own, which distracts from the pursuit of your original business proposition. Secondly, when those pursuits are successful, outside leadership is then imposed on company operations until the debt is repaid. Mr. Zwilling's article – and countless tales from history, including the famous one about the Wright brothers' achievements in flight – also underscore the critical results that can arise from having to rely on ingenuity, perseverance, and resourcefulness in building a business venture, compared with the relative ease of spending someone else's money.

For these and other reasons, I believe in self-financing, which for the record does include the use of banks, savings, and a couple of credit cards, in my case. Where my business is concerned, there is a convenience factor involved in being able to swipe a card for expenses, have the credit card company tally what I owe and then send me a bill for payment. For that convenience, I pay some minor fees – and finance charges for unpaid balances. These tools and others, like a home-equity line of credit, also give me a means for financing substantial purchases or unforeseen expenses as needs arise. Clearly, anticipating cost issues and having a plan for dealing with them may be the difference in breaking or making a business.

On the other hand, even for solitary consulting operations, consultant, speaker, and bestselling author Alan Weiss, Ph.D., advises proprietors to secure a year's worth of expenses prior to starting their businesses.[2] His counsel is detailed, wise, and proven to be effective in thousands of applications ... so when he says it may take a new consultant six to 12 months to get her practice going, that insight is bankable. Most consultants can get by on less money than ventures involving more than one person, and Dr. Weiss's suggestions for outside financing list family members as being more ideal than other investors.

Having started with a basic desire to make money, keep control, and avoid debt, the needs to address cost issues and build-up a successful operation present two very real situations where outside financial resources are potential lifesavers. With more ambitious businesses, the needs grow proportionally ...

thereby validating the importance of investors who can offer means for dealing with costs beyond your personal savings and credit cards.

Investors

Before examining the types of investors and the investment landscape, I feel compelled to share the insights of serial entrepreneur and investor Faisal Hoque from his 2014 article in Fast Company.[3] According to him, for anyone planning to use outside capital, evaluating potential investors is of the utmost importance.

While some business ventures attract investors, most require a dedicated, proactive diligence. Heeding Mr. Hoque's warning, investor scrutiny is strongly advised. The footnotes on UpCounsel's guide to investors deserve careful consideration, encouraging us to first assess every possible aspect of the history and reputation of all those we might accept money from. If any lawsuits connect with a potential investor, consider turning elsewhere. Other basic questions include, is your investor seeking to get in and out quickly, and how exactly do they benefit from their relationship with you?

Across the spectrum of investor types, which can range from personal and angel investors to "crowd" or peer-to-peer lenders, venture capitalists and banks, there are varying requirements regarding how one applies for the right to borrow money, and in the ways the investment deal will be structured and governed.[4] If you will exclusively make payments against your loan, you are borrowing money on a debt basis ... but if the investment is based on a percentage of company ownership, you are then trading your equity in exchange for funding. The latter structure is standard in dealing with VCs, which generally seek to invest large sums of money over a few years in order to build large-scale companies that are highly profitable. If a VC-funded venture goes public, the VC firm can exit the investment with a massive financial windfall. As explained in the following video by Evan Carmichael, investments might also be made based on convertible debt (debt-based at first, but investors can change to equity basis if they choose), on payment of royalties as a percentage of sales, or some combination of the above.

- Investor Pitch – How much should an investor get? https://youtu.be/NSUpjsw9Ico[5]

Based on guidance from my CPA when I originally incorporated Darnell Works, Inc., the articles of incorporation specified 100 shares of capital stock. That stock would come into play in the event I decided to accept money against company equity, instead of simply repaying it with interest.

Another fundraising avenue available to us all is crowdfunding, where money can be raised through the public, essentially by using the internet to explain one's needs and offering rewards or returns that encourage even small financial contributions. From GoFundMe to Indiegogo, Kickstarter and many other platforms, the direct appeal to the public can pay massive rewards for savvy communicators. The popularity of this approach and the hundreds of billions of dollars that individuals and companies have raised by using it make it clear that crowdfunding is well worth considering. I can also add this, based on my personal experience: Like all the other strategies for raising investments, building, and managing crowdfunding campaigns and dealing with "crowdfunders" represents a very resource-intensive initiative, requiring vast commitments and dedication, even when they are not successful.

With this quick survey of investors, I am sure you can see that engagement and communications are keys even in the basic preparations for a company to be ready to begin pursuing them. The ground is fertile for communications professionals who understand leadership, management, profitability … and storytelling.

Financial Objectives

Once again, for anyone thinking about accepting outside investments, the importance of thoroughly vetting potential investors as agreeable people to work with, who can bring valuable experience to bear and offer wise, supportive counsel, cannot be overstated. Beyond that, since the business nature of the agreement can have dire consequences, the structure of the funding also demands close examination.

In March 2014, entrepreneur Clay Olivier was the CEO of Volusion, Inc., where he had helped to build it up from one employee and revenue of U.S. $100,000 to 500 employees and revenue of U.S. $60 million. At that time, he contributed an article to The Next Web entitled "To accept funding or not."[6] The next January, Volusion completed a U.S. $55 million Series A round of equity financing, as reported by the Austin Business Journal (ABJ). Worth noting, in December 2015, ABJ reported that Mr. Olivier had quietly exited the company. To me, that backstory adds more dimension to the insights shared in The Next Web article.

After explaining all the hard work that went into building the company up prior to exploring outside financing, and making a solid case for the benefits of postponing the pursuit of investors as long as possible, Mr. Olivier then dives into the question of debt versus equity financing. Another article is referenced there, on the subject of <u>valuation</u> ... where George Deeb of Red Rocket Ventures guides readers on the means for establishing how much a company is worth, so it can be presented to investors.[7]

Further analyzing Mr. Olivier's account, factors in determining investor compensation generally include the amount of money being raised, the stock being issued, and the company's valuation. In his example they might want at least one-fifth of the equity, with a dividend greater than seven percent on top. Obviously, that formula could erase any owner profit when the company sells or liquidates.

Faisal Hoque's earlier referenced Fast Company story addresses the idea that a strong valuation helps shield control from outside investors. However, after asserting that most funding structures use either "preferred shares" (as opposed to common stock) or "convertible debt," Mr. Hoque confesses that in separate situations, he lost control of companies due to issues related to preferred stock and convertible debt, respectively.

One might easily wonder about the details of Mr. Olivier's quiet departure from Volusion. In any case, there is plenty of evidence pointing to the importance of negotiating fair and equitable funding structures in the pursuit of a company's financial objectives. Failing to arrange the details shrewdly can kill your company or hand its control to your investors.

The Big Deal: Going Public

Consider this: Despite only one percent of U.S. businesses being publicly traded,[8] only two privately held companies (Ikea and Lego Group) scored top 10 status in the 2018 YouGov Global Brand Health Rankings. That YouGov distinction confers great honor to some of the world's most prominent public companies, including Google, YouTube, Samsung, Facebook, and Amazon. After YouGov's 2018 report was published, an executive for YouTube said the rankings prove that relationships between business success, news coverage, and brand health are intricate.[9]

When individuals decide to form a company, one of the necessities is the protection of personal assets secured by establishing a C or S corporation, or an LLC. There are laws governing the procedures for launching even the smallest business, and those typically mandate the need for establishing and involving one or more directors. If you are prepared to turn this relatively easy-to-manage function of formally engaging business counselors into a veritable academic institution, that is just one of the feats necessary to prepare a company to go public.

Building a board of directors that is actively involved with a company's governance, and that will meet all of the actual requirements of the Securities and Exchange Commission (SEC), represents the fourth of 16 steps that Andreessen Horowitz General Partner Jeff Jordan recommends CEOs complete before taking their ventures public – or in other words, filing for an Initial Public Offering (IPO).[10] The first steps involve absolute mastery of the firm's financial functions under the leadership of an astute Chief Financial Officer (CFO). Beyond building the right board, Mr. Jordan advises forging solid relationships with bankers, investors, and every company stakeholder. His eighth item in order of importance, placed before governance, accounting, profitability, planning, and positioning, is to diligently conduct a company-wide communications campaign relating plans for the IPO.

Why would a CEO and his supporting team in a corporate venture decide to go public? Writing for InvestorPlace.com, Tom Taulli says it is mostly about the money, but not entirely.[11] Beyond the monetary potential (usually U.S. $100–150 million is raised), going public allows stock to be used to acquire other companies, stockholders can easily exchange their holdings for money, and the company's public perception skyrockets.

Remembering the mission of this book – to help you home-in on a communications skill set you can use to create value for others – Mr. Taulli's insights make it clear that completing an IPO is tougher than ever. To be successful, companies must build and maintain communications systems which themselves require millions of dollars in annual investments.

Complying with such stringent regulations and proactively developing interest in a venture's stocks are the standards for companies seeking to operate at the highest levels. Sounds like a job for superior communications experts, right?

Why Is IR the Highest Level of PR?

From David C. Baker and Blair Enns, I learned that when a company positions itself around its expertise, it can then charge more for its services. Year after year, salary surveys confirm that individuals who specialize in IR are consistently among the highest paid in the field of public relations. According to Dennis Wilcox, Ph.D., and Glen Cameron, Ph.D., in their book

"Public Relations Strategies and Tactics," there are many reasons for this.[12] First, IR professionals need to be experts in communications – but also in the field of finance, so they can intelligently illuminate a company's prospects for investors. Also, they must be able to deftly educate their clients' publics according to SEC guidelines on issues spanning accounting, mergers, IPOs, financial reporting, and other public disclosures.

Obviously, among those publics are analysts, stockbrokers, individual and institutional investors, and the hypervigilant financial and business press. Given their in-depth first-hand knowledge and proficiency conveying numbers and their meanings, any and all official company analyses, reports, and presentations are sure to originate with a team of astute IR pros.

Clearly, in companies that are publicly held – or even private companies that are regularly dealing with investors – the communications counsel holds a great deal of influence. For most of the companies I have worked for, engaging professional communications counsel is not common practice. So long as a company is profitable and business is going smoothly, having a PR consultant onboard is often seen as a luxury. However, when a company has stockholders and/or outside investors, there is a bona fide need to diligently communicate what is happening, including the company's financial situation. These communications need to be intelligent, shrewd, and truthful, especially when the company is publicly traded.

- Today's Investor Relations: An Art or Science? https://youtu.be/7qxdDB9qpNs

IR professionals, the company executives they support, and all of those who encounter the materials they produce together, rely on the reporting to be factual. The consequences for false or even misleading communications can cause businesses and investments to fail, and they can be considered criminal where publicly traded companies and the SEC are involved.

To further illustrate the importance of IR, imagine this: What would happen if a large, publicly traded company decided to reverse its controversial position after many years, to take responsibility for a disastrous accident that killed thousands of people and harmed half a million others, and finally offer to provide substantial financial support to all the victims? In 2004, thanks to the Yes Men group of online activists specializing in parodying the questionable ethics of large-scale enterprises, the BBC aired an interview on the 20th anniversary of the industrial disaster at the Union Carbide factory in Bhopal, India. In that story, a man claiming to be a spokesperson for Dow

Chemical (which owns Union Carbide) said that Dow would finally accept responsibility and provide billions of dollars in much-needed financial aid for the victims of the disaster.[13] The consequences of this inconceivable ruse were immediate: According to CNN, within hours of the BBC airing its story, Dow's share price fell 4.24 percent, reducing its market value by U.S. $2 billion. Quickly after the BBC issued an apology and exposed the story as a hoax, Dow's share price corrected, and its losses were recovered. In India, those who momentarily rejoiced were crushed to learn the truth, and elsewhere around the world, media organizations and those who rely on them were left discussing the Yes Men and their controversial tactics, but also, the Bhopal disaster, the lingering devastation, and Dow's official position claiming zero responsibility.

Foundations of IR

Even that single case demonstrating the high stakes of communications pertaining to a publicly traded company provides solid evidence for the vital importance of IR. In America and beyond, research into this revered field of expertise leads to the National Investor Relations Institute (NIRI). Since 1969, this professional association of corporate officers and IR consultants responsible for communications among corporate management, shareholders, securities analysts, and other financial community constituents has become the world's largest professional IR association. Today, NIRI members represent thousands of publicly held companies representing trillions of dollars in stock-market capitalization.

In its constant quest to advance IR practices and the competency and stature of its members, NIRI's dedication to establishing standards and to education on IR practices has proven to be comprehensive. Consider its Investor Relations Charter™ (IRC) Competency Framework, which consists of these ten core competency domains: IR Strategy Formulation; IR Planning, Implementation and Measurement; Corporate Messaging Development; Marketing and Outreach; Corporate Financial Reporting and Analysis; Business Insight; Strategic Counsel and Collaboration; Capital Markets and Capital Structure; Corporate Regulatory Compliance; and Corporate Governance.[14]

On its own, this framework provides a master plan for corporate communications at the highest level. IRC certification is the organization's first professional credential. Overall, earning and maintaining that credential involves meeting educational and professional experience requirements, adhering to the IRC Code of Conduct and to NIRI's Code of Ethics, passing the IRC exam, and participating in ongoing professional development activities.

Twice per year, NIRI presents its "Fundamentals of Investor Relations and Service Provider Showcase" training events. The curriculum is designed to correspond to the 10 core domains of the IRC Competency Framework, and its completion contributes to the IRC Program's educational prerequisites. Participation in any of these events adds far-reaching and immensely valuable experience for communications consultants at all levels.

Exploration

1. Imagine a problem you must solve in your business. What are the advantages or disadvantages of having money to spend to solve the problem when that money must be paid back?
2. As a consultant, how can you prepare financially to deal with unforeseen expenses and business development challenges? Tip: Alan Weiss's book "Getting Started in Consulting" offers a lot of sage advice.
3. List three reasons why a family member may be the best early investor in your company – and three more reasons why you may be better off using a bank.
4. List three reasons to stick with debt financing for a business – and three more reasons for using equity financing instead.
5. If you had to pick either convertible debt or royalties as your basis for receiving an investment, which do you feel is riskier for you? Explain your answer.
6. Set up accounts on Kickstarter, Indiegogo, and GoFundMe, and make a small contribution to a campaign for any of these accounts you have never used before, so you can better understand how each one works. To gain experience, consider mounting and running a campaign for someone you know, on a pro-bono or project basis, perhaps based on a share of royalties.
7. Your clients begin pursuing investors and ask how you can help. What do you say?
8. Your clients tell you they now have new investors. What do you do?
9. Your clients tell you they want to grow their business and possibly go public. How can you help?
10. From the story on Dow Chemical and the Yes Men, which of those two groups would you rather work for? My advice: Honor your heart's answer to this question as you pursue your career in the field of communications.

Notes

1. Zwilling, M. (2016, September 1). Smart Entrepreneurs Build Startups Without Investors. Forbes. http://bit.ly/startDIY
2. Weiss, A. (2009). *Getting Started in Consulting* (3rd ed.). Wiley.
3. Hoque, F. (2014, December 16). What Every Entrepreneur Should Know Before Taking Any Outside Investment. Fast Company. http://bit.ly/TIPFstrct
4. Types of Investors: Everything You Need to Know. (n.d.). UpCounsel. Retrieved May 17, 2021, from https://www.upcounsel.com/types-of-investors
5. Evan Carmichael. (2014, August 20). Investor Pitch – How much should an investor get? [Video]. https://youtu.be/NSUpjsw9Ico
6. Olivier, C. (2014, March 4). To Accept Funding Or Not? The Tipping Point for Taking Outside Investment. TNW | Entrepreneur. http://bit.ly/TIP-pnt
7. Deeb, G. (2016, March 23). Looking for Investors? Here's How to Value Your Startup. TNW | Entrepreneur. http://bit.ly/TIPvlue
8. Biery, M. E. (2013, June 7). 4 Things You Don't Know About Private Companies. Forbes. http://bit.ly/4privCos
9. Gwynn, S. (2018, August 2). Facebook Falls in BrandIndex Global Brand Health Ranking. Campaign Live. http://bit.ly/YG18camp
10. Jordan, J. (2017, August 22). 16 Things CEOs Should do Before an IPO. TechCrunch. http://tcrn.ch/2vlqlfA
11. Taulli, T. (2016, March 6). 4 Reasons Companies Go Public. InvestorPlace. https://investorplace.com/?p=128884
12. Wilcox, D. L., & Cameron, G. T. (2011). *Public Relations: Strategies and Tactics* (10th ed.). Pearson.
13. BBC Tricked: The Yes Men Apologize For Bhopal Tragedy Because Dow Chemical Won't : (2004, December 3). Indybay. http://bit.ly/YESmBho
14. Investor Relations Charter Competency Framework. (2015, January). National Investor Relations Institute. http://bit.ly/2OO76po

4
Advanced PR Account Management

At last, we are ready to focus on generating media exposure for your clients. Being able to convince journalists that your clients are worthy subjects requires a great deal of diligence, hence all the buildup. When everything works and you get the interview, or content you have authored and distributed is used in some media outlet, or your client's social media feeds successfully attract inbound business opportunities, you will probably be fulfilling the gist of the mission you were hired to address.

Early in my career when I was employed to write for Century III at Universal Studios, that was an opportunity to author the stories my boss had determined would make good, strategic news content she could use to address her objectives. Through those endeavors and others that followed where it became my job to determine both what the stories should be and how they would be used, the challenges a company faces in intelligently leveraging these communications activities became clearer to me.

In this chapter, we will examine the elements of the successful news bureau, where PR programs fulfill incredibly important, cross-company missions … through to the point of seeing exactly how the desired results can be achieved and maximized. We will then expand into the related world of content marketing, with a discussion on expertly planning and managing those activities, as well as both internal and external events.

The Integrated News Bureau

For all of us caught up in marketing today, we must be ready to address the subject of Return on Investment (ROI). On the bottom line, every marketing expenditure's returns must justify its costs. Most people who have worked in businesses that embrace PR seem to endorse its viability. As evidence, consider the example provided by Molly (Borchers) Beane, the founder and CEO of the all-natural beauty and lifestyle brand, From Molly with Love. Worth mentioning, Ms. Beane's professional PR experience spans top-level PR firms and the U.S. Department of Energy, and she is certified in the practices of PR measurement and evaluation. In a 2014 story in Huffington Post, she cited increased credibility, web traffic, and new business opportunities as specific benefits of media exposure.[1]

A 2017 article entitled "Myth: PR Campaigns Can't Be Measured" by International Marketing and PR Manager Doreen Clark (Pierce) added more evidence. Reiterating the benefits listed by Ms. Beane, she confirmed PR's positive impacts on bolstering brands, raising profiles, and expanding relationships. To her, PR drives marketing's impact to higher levels, and the many viable means for measuring it include tracking and evaluating social media metrics and seeing how results impact issues like market share.[2]

The results of Ms. Beane's Huffington Post survey of five PR industry leaders asking specifically about the keys to measuring the ROI of Public Relations lead us to a place I am well familiar with; since the meaning of "public relations" can be confusing to some people, to boil it down, I often begin by talking about objectives. More specifically, I will ask what someone wishes to accomplish, and why. Once those questions are answered and prioritized in our To-Do list, we then can devise strategies ... then move into tactics aimed toward achieving our desired results in the best ways possible.

Ms. Beane's interview subjects illuminate these PR measurement insights from experts: (1) begin with objectives; (2) agree on how PR efforts will be measured; (3) compare your results with those of your competitors; (4) measure impacts across the entire marketing spectrum (sales, customer service, etc.); (5) use social media for listening, not just broadcasting; and (6) commit on an ongoing basis and use the results to learn and improve.

That Huffington Post article ends with an anecdote about a story's publication leading to a line out the door for the company it was written about. Ms. Beane also refers to two other important sets of PR measures that are worth discussing here. The first is Advertising Value Equivalency, or AVE, which is widely considered to be outdated, despite sustained use. During my time at The Terpin Group (TTG), this approach validated our monthly reports, comparing the amount of editorial space generated for our clients to the same amount of advertising space. For example, for an eight-minute radio interview for one of my TTG clients in 1999, the value was computed to be U.S. $4,250, based on the media outlet's advertising rate for the same amount of time. The reach for that broadcast was 100,000 people – and that is another factor we reported to our client, while clarifying that, generally, PR exposure's value exceeds that of advertising, due to it carrying the implied endorsement from the media outlet.

Over time, seeking more objective-driven and evidence-based evaluation than AVEs can offer, various groups including the International Association for Measurement and Evaluation of Communication (AMEC) have promoted new standards, known as the Barcelona Principles.[3] First introduced in 2010, AMEC updated its platform in 2015, as follows.

- Goal setting and measurement are fundamental to communication and public relations.
- Measuring communication outcomes is recommended versus only measuring outputs.
- The effect on organizational performance can and should be measured where possible.
- Measurement and evaluation require both qualitative and quantitative methods.
- AVEs do not accurately convey communication values.
- Social media can and should be measured consistently with other media channels.
- Measurement and evaluation should be transparent, consistent, and valid.

Back in the mid-1990s, seeing these changes coming, some wise communications professionals at the University of Indiana set out to put their acclaimed news bureau on the right track for the future. It is fascinating to read the detailed account of this development from the late Christopher Simpson, who went on to launch SimpsonScarborough, a marketing research and strategy firm specializing in higher education. Writing for CASE Currents Magazine, his story entitled "The Day We Closed the News Bureau," chronicled the university's high-stakes maneuverings to switch from a purely promotions-oriented PR strategy to one built on integrated marketing.[4]

After intelligently building the case for the new paradigm, Mr. Simpson presented six steps for instituting integrated marketing. I still find the approach to be highly sound.

1. Determine what audience you wish to target.
2. Evaluate those individuals' desires and the problems they face.
3. Based on your assessments, design a campaign that is sure to please.
4. In your messaging, be creative and aim for effectiveness.
5. Communicate proactively.
6. Measure your success in altering mindsets among your target audience.

Here, I hope you will find the terrain to be familiar. Instead of presenting this chapter simply to ignite our efforts to launch your career as a communications consultant, we have advanced from a common foundation uniting solid leadership, creativity, design thinking, branding, integrated marketing, and customer service. Knowing the importance of strategic promotion, these new lessons courtesy of Ms. Beane, Ms. Clark, Mr. Simpson, and their peers driving AMEC spur us to approach our communications methodically, and adjust as we go, to ensure success. Adopting all this knowledge and leveraging these insights, our efforts are sure to propel the desired results – and maximize ROI in the process.

Making News, Strategically: Your Media List

In Mr. Simpson's chronicle about the University of Indiana's paradigm shift, what replaced the news bureau was the Office of Communications and Marketing. Based upon that solid case study for the need to marry marketing to communications, let's proceed into the media relations process.

Clearly, strategically sound communications programs are highly attuned to the "wants and needs" of the audiences they are intended for. This critical focus culminates in media planning, where media contacts (reporters, editors, analysts, and influencers) are identified and sorted (or segmented) according to their relevance, reach and influence over our target audiences. In my efforts for my clients, I tend to see the media as the VIP audience I exist to serve, fully understanding that they, in turn, serve their audiences. Regarding these super-important media luminaries, I often refer to this spectrum in helping my clients understand the risks and rewards, set their sights accordingly, and establish their communications goals intelligently (Figure 2).

Figure 2: Media View Spectrum[5]

Source: Darnell, R. (2021, May 25). Media View Spectrum (Illustration). Darnell Works. https://www.darnellworks.com

To explain the risk element, breaking news outlets are the world's news programs, newspapers and news magazines. Trade news outlets are those publications that cover specialty niches within industries. The advertising sector has its news outlets (Ad Age, Adweek, Campaign, Digiday, The Drum) but also many trade publications covering creativity, production, graphic design, etc. On the left side of the spectrum, breaking news reporters will present the news as they see it, and if it makes a company or a subject look bad, so it goes. In my college studies, I learned about a seminal newsroom editorial value, which says a lot about the media's – and the audiences' – appetite: "If it bleeds, it leads." Across the spectrum of premier media outlets, dirt remains highly prized, and failures command attention, where a company's good news is often ignored.

On the trade news side, there is usually a greater willingness to focus on positive news – meaning that the doors stand more open to PR practitioners and their "good news" stories. While there are exceptions, I still emphasize the merits of storytelling on the trade side of the spectrum, where news has greater likelihood of appearing with its strategic messaging intact. While breaking news outlets (with their massive audiences) are often seen as more desirable, the risks are much higher.

Focusing on analysts and influencers represents highly strategic PR specialization. Many analysts are regularly engaged in ongoing research, leading to original studies and reports that are widely used among business executives for intelligence. Some analysts also publish articles on media platforms like Inc., Huffington Post, and Forbes. As such, I view them as a special breed of journalists, and for those who are well established in a niche where a client has news, I include them in my outreach. That also applies to influencers.

- Including influencers in your media relations activities is shrewd. This story illuminates the more specific practice of executing an influencer marketing campaign: http://bit.ly/2Up2bOL[6]

For your media relations efforts, compile a list of media targets that addresses the entire spectrum of outlets where your news might be considered relevant. Many services exist that allow you to purchase contact information: In my professional opinion, the better approach is to do your homework in the form of your own research – to investigate who has reported on a company and its competitors and gather executive input on media outlets of interest. Typically, media outlets overtly list their staff members and contact information on their websites. By using Twitter for research, chances are good for finding writers, reporters and editors who are open to direct messages.

In the past, most magazines provided editorial calendars as a part of their media kits, as much for use by advertising as for PR planners. While they are increasingly rare, it is wise to attempt to track them down for any magazine you are aiming to pitch. Not only do they tell you what the editors are interested in covering in the future, they also provide submission deadlines and other key details. If you are lucky to find numerous relevant publications that publish editorial calendars, you can use that information to develop a media relations plan that will be of great use in helping you achieve targeted editorial coverage over time.

Without that type of roadmap available to match your news developments with the known interests of working members of the media, you are left to your diligence in research and analysis, and your instincts. Who might like to hear about what is happening at your client company, and how can you present that news in a way that will lead them to cover it favorably?

Among all the other relevant factors here, timing is critical. Think about it: To achieve success, you must professionally present information that qualifies as "news" to journalists who must assess – and potentially report on, edit, and publish it, under their name – on a timeline (which varies by media type and even a given journalist's workload) that can deploy a story while it is still *news*. Never underestimate the value of time in your media relations efforts: With enough of it, the home run feature story is possible. On the other hand, if your story is about something that happened last week, pitching it as news to breaking news outlets could tarnish your reputation.

Also, remember the lessons arising from these types of interactions can open important doors to working relationships that can be amazingly fruitful over time. Indeed, the relationships you build as your career progresses are likely to drive your value exponentially. The same is true for your knowledge of media outlets: From TV, podcasts and radio to magazines and blogs, embrace the need to fully educate yourself about them and their particulars. This aspect of your expertise is premium rocket fuel for your success in this field.

- As just one example of the depth of knowledge required to successfully interface with the media at-large – or even just one media outlet in particular – I suggest you fully explore this "How to get TechCrunch to cover your startup" thread on Quora.com, and take notes: http://bit.ly/TCcovet.[7] Many posted comments disagree with others; bear in mind that everything you read might be true in different scenarios.

Preparing to Pitch

In my proposal, I list these functions of the news bureau: Generate news releases to promote new developments, strengthen client/vendor alliances and provide a flow of strategic information about your developments and major activities to key media outlets; develop/refine media kits, including company backgrounders, bios, press releases and media alerts.

Interestingly, everything mentioned there involves research and writing, and the importance of strategy cannot be overstated in making these preparations (Figure 3).

- News release, press release, social media release: I tend to describe regular announcements intended for media distribution as news releases. This puts the emphasis on "news," while also addressing the fact that such stories are intended for more than just media relations. Social media releases more formally skew away from the fact-based structure of a news release (where according to the "inverted pyramid" approach,[8] the most important details appear at the top of the story), to appeal directly to mainstream readers who are probably not official members of the press. Each of these "releases" (stories) is also accompanied by images and relevant audiovisual assets, provided in a way that makes it easy for media pros to collect and use them in their reporting, as they choose.

Figure 3: Inverted Pyramid

Source: The Air Force Departmental Publishing Office (AFDPO). (2011, January 24). Inverted pyramid [Illustration]. Wikipedia. http://bit.ly/INVpyr

- Company backgrounder: Especially when your clients are interested in attracting investors, this document telling the story of a company from its inception through the present is a standard component of a media kit. Typically, it closely matches the "About" section on a company website, and will include biographical details of company principals, and a timeline noting key historical developments from the company's origination onward.
- Bios and headshots: Well-written bios are essential for many aspects of corporate communications. There are more applications for brief bios,

although long ones also have important uses. Bios can begin with the present and trace back to a person's origins or start at the beginning and bridge to their current situation. Complete bios also include an up-to-date, high quality headshot photo that is readily accessible for media usage.

- Media alert: This specific type of press release communicates the bullet points Who, What, Where, When and Why. It is meant to inform working members of the press of a newsworthy development coming up at a particular time and location, with all the details necessary to allow media outlets to dispatch camera crews and/or reporters, and to contact sources for more detailed information and arrange interviews.
- Media kit or press kit: You will often find all the above contained within the Electronic Press Kit (EPK) websites I create and maintain for my clients. Another component I add as time and budgets allow is a listing of media coverage, with the most recent stories at the top. The coverage listing is important for many reasons: It is a key source of ROI for my clients; preparing it allows me to quickly see and communicate what is most interesting about my clients; it is also extremely valuable to all stakeholders for my client companies, as well as to diligent journalists who want to assess the company's newsworthiness. Having all this information and media assets highly organized in one place is a key to passing the lightning-speed litmus test most journalists conduct as they consider a story.

News Release Development, Strategy, Pitching, and Distribution

As mentioned in the previous chapter's introduction, when you pitch a company and its stories to journalists, the words that meaningfully set the venture apart (its positioning) either prove successful by earning the desired results, or otherwise. Soon thereafter, we also explored the elevator pitch, and I suggested you watch Entrepreneur Magazine's series "Elevator Pitch" to see the importance of a key message in presenting a business venture. On that show, if the short pitch generates interest among the potential investors, the elevator doors open to the board room, and if they don't, it is game over.

Let's drill further into the idea of getting news out to the world, and also, trying to get journalists to cover it in a positive way. This story from publicity expert Joan Stewart is highly illuminating. I invite you to read on, to see how she applies our key skill set (Account Management; Customer Service; Planning; Writing; Media Relations; Measurement; Reporting) to something very practical, using shrewd media relations tactics.

- How to Publicize a Garden Walk and Other Local Events: http://ow.ly/pOhH30dHOuv[9]

Having worked with publicists for major rock stars and leading brands, I view the diligence, professionalism and drive for success displayed and shared by Ms. Stewart as essential ingredients for producing exceptional, marketing-driven media coverage. She begins with researching her client and its media universe extensively, defining objectives (attracting "sell-out crowds"), and then discussing media relations tactics (pitches, news releases, flyers, photography, signage, community relations, couponing, social media) that exemplify integrated marketing while showing exactly how and where PR tactics fit in.

In the same way that Ms. Stewart's coupons and other pieces all fit together in her campaign, your news release, and other elements of what you will share with the media (photos, videos, bios, backgrounders) all are intended to drive the objective (perhaps: getting prominent media to report on your news in a positive way). Using a copy platform, specify the Client, Objectives, Target Audience, Sales Theme, Bonus Items, Positioning and Approach for your story, and then formulate your storytelling accordingly. For a news release, follow the inverted pyramid approach; if you see the story more as a social media release (less "news" value from the media's perspective), spend more time writing the lead paragraph in the style of a feature story.

There is a lot of craftsmanship involved in writing powerful, communicative headlines that aptly introduce and encapsulate the subject matter to follow. Writing a headline that is not summarily explained by the story it introduces is a good way to lose your audience, potentially for life. Based on my experience, I always advise my clients to consider using long headlines, since oftentimes, that is all anyone will read.

Any company news release needs executive approval – ideally by those who run the company or companies involved. When a story goes out to the media, or is posted for release, that makes it fair game for anyone to report on. Imagine something you mention in a story resulting in an angry call from another company's CEO or lawyer, asking who gave you permission to talk to the media about them; that is a very real prospect for any of the details your story includes. As such, handle with care, get approvals, and if possible, have stories reviewed by the company's investor relations and/or legal counselors, prior to putting anything out.

Next comes your media strategy. Assuming that time is on your side, you have three main options for how you send your story to the media: You can pitch it as an exclusive, you can send it out in advance of its release date (possibly under embargo), and/or you can put it out widely to everyone at the same time, possibly using a newswire. Before we explore those approaches further, let's reassess your media list and put some additional thought toward its strategic usage.

Your media list should include the journalists and editors who cover the region(s) where your client is based, but also those who write about the niches and nuances of the types of activities where your client is aiming to achieve success. There is your "master" media list for developments of a larger scale (new product, major project award or development, company expansion), and variations for occurrences like new hires, events, passion projects among staff, etc. It is important to include targets at the top of your master list who may prove to be impossible to reach, but who represent the home run everyone aspires to hit through your efforts. For many years, for most of my clients and their clients, this was a single person: Stuart Elliott, who wrote the Advertising column for The New York Times. Put your Stuart Elliott at the top of your master list, and then work your way down with others comprising your wish list appearing in priority order … down to the list of people you are most sure your news may interest, including any paid newswires or placements.

With that list in good shape, you are ready to proceed in building your strategy.

The Non-Paid Editorial Exclusive

Offering an "exclusive" is a great way to gain the attention of a working journalist. However, you must also consider factors like these: not every story is worthy of being offered as an exclusive; having a journalist respond with interest does not guarantee that a story will come out, nor that it will be positive; understanding what is meant by an exclusive is imperative.

In a thoughtful story on this subject, Richard Etchison of Crenshaw Communications writes, "An exclusive typically means offering a key tidbit, news item, or interview to a single journalist with the understanding that he or she will be first. The story can then be released to other media after the exclusive runs."[10] While that's all true, there are nuances to consider. A key to successfully leveraging the power of the exclusive is to remember that you are building relationships with VIP journalists on behalf of your clients. When you enter a discussion of this type, you are committing to giving the journalist full access to everything you can offer for your story for a certain amount of time, and you are hoping for a lot: A positive story that is well placed (if it is for a magazine, will it be positioned prominently?), well-researched, written and edited, and comes out relatively quickly. Of course, these are the same things you are hoping for with any coverage, but exclusives offer the best chances for you to generate substantial coverage where you have some control over those details.

If you engage a journalist with your offer for an exclusive, that development becomes the most important factor in that media relations strategy, right up until it publishes, and immediately afterward. With all media relations results set to build upon the success of that first coverage, and so much invested into that relationship, promoting that placement across all platforms is the next order of business. While I do agree that the news release written to land the exclusive can then be released to other media outlets, I suggest holding it up by about 24 hours, out of respect to your first responder. From there, respectfulness toward others you pitch your story to involves informing them about the exclusive, too, with language like this: "The Wall Street Journal broke this story for us yesterday (share the link), but we wanted you to see it as well."

After making my appeal to my top contact for an exclusive, waiting to hear back in the allotted time I have given them and perhaps circling back once before its expiration, I then inform my contact of my intentions to move on with the exclusive pitching. So long as the story remains interesting and is not yet public, you can continue to work your way down your list of media contacts, offering the exclusive to one after another, professionally and diplomatically. Hopefully, sooner or later, a story appears.

Wide News Release Distribution

Perhaps time is short for getting a story out, or for some other reason, you opt out of exclusive pitching, so you are ready to send the story out to the world. For anyone on your media list, if they are going to receive the news from and build a relationship with you, you must contact them in a meaningful way <u>before</u> everyone else in the world can read your breaking news. This contact can be by telephone, email, social media, or your choice combination. In my experience, email is generally superior, but using it effectively does involve being prepared to add use of the telephone and other suitable means of communication, when you get a favorable response.

At this stage in your media planning, you must know how you intend to see your distribution all the way through. Options include: (1) placing an exclusive around a release and considering the job done; (2) continuing to pitch a release after an exclusive has published – or on a non-exclusive basis; and (3) putting the story out on a newswire and/or a company's website/blog/social media. Without taking step 3, your "news" may remain a secret (if you earn no coverage); however, once you take it, the opportunities around earned media coverage change. Immediately after step 3 occurs, the story's value peaks, and it then becomes more of a talking point for newer developments to build upon as time moves on.

The importance of "releasing" news with as much prestige as possible often leads to distribution of your story (and other elements of your package) over a newswire. The two leading newswire services are operated by Business Wire and PR Newswire (PRN, now Cision), respectively, and another popular choice is PRWeb.com (now owned by Cision). These companies operate the well distributed media "tickers" venerable newsrooms monitor for major stories. My experience using PRN goes back to my days at TTG, and I have found that using it for distribution has many legitimate and worthwhile benefits. First among those, there certainly is a prestige factor for companies willing to pay for newswire distribution, and the resulting benefit of having an archive of professionally packaged news stories appearing in the world via newswire syndication has cache. However, I see newswire distribution more as an endgame than a means for generating earned media exposure.

In other words, newswire distribution is one of many placement strategies that PR practitioners can use to generate paid (not earned) editorial coverage. In this paid category, your media list should also take opportunities like these into account: blogs published by membership- or directory-based organizations and websites; the "branded content" agencies materializing from inside major media outlets which accept money to author and publish advertorial content; all other creative and paid promotional initiatives that can engage targeted audiences with your story package on social media, websites, and search engines.

The time before you use any paid means for distributing your story to the public is likely to be your last opportunity to use it to interest working journalists; after it has been distributed widely, your journalist friends will probably lose interest. Now that you are ready to pitch your story to them, remember all the ground we have covered, seize the moment, and pique interest.

1. Make your pitch respectful, short, and highly engaging.
2. Let your contact know the status of the story – if it will be distributed over a newswire, tell them when, so they know how much time they have before the news is out widely.

3. Another tactic you can use to potentially raise more interest among journalists is to place an embargo on the news, stating that the story must remain confidential until a future point in time (usually at least a day). If the story is embargoed, quickly address that in your pitch.
4. Offer accompanying elements, photos, bios, backgrounders, as simply and elegantly as possible (for example, EPK site on one link).
5. Either provide the full story or offer to send the story upon request.
6. Be ready to follow-up as the embargo time/day approaches ... but for any given pitch, never follow-up with a non-responsive journalist more than twice.
7. If/when you hear from a journalist, drop everything to get them whatever they need.
8. Search for coverage and give any pickups prominent attention on owned and social media.

Interviews

When a pitch is successful, media contacts often express interest in arranging an interview as quickly as possible. You can expect them to want to speak with the most important person involved in your story. In the creative industry, it is not uncommon for the reporters to want to speak with my client's client. That wish is a good one to honor, if your client supports it. Otherwise, your task is to arrange for your client's chosen executive to be the subject of the interview, if possible. In the event no executive is available, you may need to field the interview yourself. In that situation, remember that if you do not want your name to appear in the coverage, you can ask to be referenced as a company spokesperson.

While interviews by phone are standard, at times they can be done over email. This guide to the media interview process relates some tips provided by the American Speech-Language-Hearing Association (ASHA).[11]

- Prepare: Ensure that the interview subject has read through the story that has been pitched to the media. You should also write-out key talking points that briefly address relevant issues pertaining to the company and the current story. In coordinating the interview, you should also request questions in advance, bearing in mind that reporters are not always able or willing to comply.
- Answer intelligently: If you do not know the answer to a question, say that. If you have information to share that you do not want to appear in the story, tell the reporter that the information is "off the record," and

ensure they agree to that before sharing. Should you simply wish to not answer a question, the correct answer is, "no comment."
- Brief, sound-bite type answers work best. Learn more about the A BEACH PRO system[12] (which stands for Analogy, Bold action words, Emotions, Examples, Attacks, Absolutes, Clichés, Humor, Pop culture references, Rhetorical questions, and Opposition quotes) from author and media training expert TJ Walker here: http://bit.ly/S_Bite.
- Stay on-topic for the story under discussion.
- Offer to provide additional information.
- You can politely ask to see the story in advance of publication to ensure accuracy, but do not insist: Media outlets are not obliged to honor that request, for various reasons.
- Once a story appears, review it quickly and provide positive feedback, even if there are problems. Then, be highly organized and respectful as you present the fewest changes possible to get the story where you want it to be.

In your role as the interview organizer, there is another important detail you should manage for any interviews that will go beyond the printed word. If your interview subject will be interviewed on TV, on the radio or for a podcast, be certain you are clear about the pronunciation of their name and the company's name, while also clarifying all other important details about the subject's core identity, including their preferred pronouns. Trust me, I have learned this lesson first-hand: After successfully lining up an interview, you do not want it to be ruined by the interviewer mispronouncing your client's name or referring to him/her in a way that disrespects them or undermines the story.

Coverage

Media coverage – with its implied endorsement of the reporting media outlet – is ideal content for social media ... particularly when it is new. Compiling media coverage and reporting that to your clients is a key step in demonstrating the ROI of your efforts, and having it appear as part of your EPK site adds to the value of your integrated newsroom. Many businesses also feature their best-earned media clippings prominently in their offices. Companies like Simply Framed make it easy to convert clippings into the type of office décor that is sure to impress all visitors: http://bit.ly/PFrames.

Simply put, when there is positive news coverage to share, doing so while it is happening and immediately afterward is of the utmost importance. Ideally, those promotions connect with every major facet of the company's marketing program, providing a talking point that is topical thanks to legitimately earning media attention. It is also extremely important to cross-promote paid media placements widely to internal and external audiences for your client. In the inevitable ROI discussions that will follow, social media statistics are sure to be examined in detail; a single "like" on Facebook can have massive consequences.

Naturally, in the spirit of building relationships with your media contacts, you want to be able to look back on the full experience of executing your media strategy and feel confident in the professionalism of your exchanges with each of them. Expressing appreciation to those who covered your news, and otherwise acknowledging their work (by Re-Tweeting their story on Twitter and/or liking their story on Facebook) are among the tools you have readily available to continue dialogues in positive ways. Most likely, you will soon be pitching these individuals again, and you always want them to know they are highly valued and respected.

Content Marketing, Social Media, and SEO

A company's owned media channels will typically include its website and possibly a blog, and from there, the social media channels where it maintains a presence. This can include LinkedIn, Facebook, and WeChat, which facilitate the publication of articles as a company or via individuals; membership or directory-based media outlets; and networks like Instagram, Pinterest, Snapchat, TikTok, and Twitter.

Again, you can and should use your earned media coverage as premium content on owned and social media channels. Furthermore, since solid media coverage is difficult and expensive to generate over time, and many company developments may not warrant the attention of news journalists, another class of storytelling subject matter has become increasingly important for companies focusing on customer relations. For sales purposes and for search engine optimization (SEO), in his book "A Website that Works," Newfangled CEO Mark O'Brien advises consistently adding strategically sound new writing to websites every month.[13] Further addressing that strategic soundness factor, Jay Baer's book "Youtility" introduces the story of River Pools and Spas to illustrate how savvy content marketing works.[14] Prior to adopting this strategy, River Pools and Spas marketed its work and its offerings on its website. Afterward, its website became a leading fiberglass swimming pool reference site. Using Mr. Baer's lexicon, this company transitioned into a "youtility" by publishing highly valuable content, not just hyping itself.

The overall need to produce original information that is organically connected to a company's purpose, values, and customers – and which is not an overt advertisement – is not new. Sponsored or branded content soared in the dawn of radio and television, strategically linking brands into the narratives of their favorite programs. There is much to know about this subject to fully harness its powers. Here are five articles illuminating the past, present, and future.

- American Press Institute, Understanding the rise of sponsored content: http://bitly.com/17VtmqP
- Mission.org, Branded Content: The What, Why, When, and How: http://bit.ly/2BivcoA
- Forbes Corporate Communications, New Study Reveals Branded Content Is Twice As Memorable As Display Ads: http://bitly.com/2CboBM4
- The DVI Group: What is branded content? http://bit.ly/2FLz8Ph
- Neil Patel, 17 Charts That Show Where Content Marketing is Heading: http://bitly.com/2OADfBv

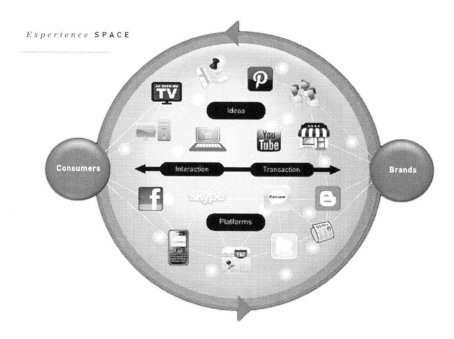

Figure 4: The Experience Space[15]

Source: Legorburu, G. and McColl, D., "Storyscaping: Stop Creating Ads, Start Creating Worlds," Wiley, April 7, 2014: http://amzn.to/1qpftnB

Drawing from The DVI Group feature,[16] branded content tells a story, it informs, and it moves the audience toward a visceral reaction. The best branded content is built around an organizing idea, which strategically facilitates consumer interactions with the brand across different platforms. Quoting The DVI Group's CEO Matthew Lopes, "We find the organizing idea at the intersection of the brand strategy/purpose, the product function, and the consumer's desires and needs. Taking these factors into account, you find the idea you can build your story around."

All of this leads us back to the place where content marketing and SEO meet. In a 2018 webinar produced by Cision and moderated by Jay Baer, Goodwill Industries International's Senior Director of Public Relations Lauren Lawson-Zilai gave a great example of the need for content marketing within her organization. While there is always diplomatic work needing to be done targeting earned media coverage, Ms. Lawson-Zilai identified a special need for strategic communications activities that focus on educating the public on the company's mission and highlighting it.[17] Goodwill created a position specifically to lead this initiative, which draws upon PR and expert usage of media on the company's internal and its social media channels. In other words, for Goodwill, there is a PR professional dedicated to using content marketing to promote the institution's mission.

Exploring that example further, a very large-scale company comprised of hundreds of independently operated stores uses a combination of communications efforts, including initiatives focusing on both earned and paid media, as well as content marketing. It is a safe bet that all efforts comply with The Barcelona Principles, and all are being measured to ensure maximum effectiveness against expenditures.

In summary, content marketing might help a non-profit illuminate its mission, it might help educate a pool company's prospects on the ins and outs of fiberglass swimming pools, it might help a brand like LEGO dramatically increase sales by building major motion pictures around its products, or it might help a PR professional like yours truly demonstrate his interests and skills in ways designed to build his reputation and awareness worldwide. Want to learn more about the world's best initiatives in this realm? Check out this story announcing winners of the 2020 Content Marketing Awards: http://bit.ly/3aqIxfN.

- To successfully engage in content marketing, extensive planning and decisive action are required. This story from HootSuite will walk you through content calendar planning: http://ow.ly/VSOt30nsh39.

Consistently publishing high quality, strategically sound content on a company's website and social media channels is just the tip of the SEO iceberg. Mr. O'Brien's "A Website that Works" walks readers through extremely specific means for ensuring websites and content are optimized for search engines, with discussions of key planning and management facets that address keywords, analytics, and much more. Many practitioners profess their expertise in this area, and it is yet another field where in-depth learning is highly advised.

In the communications programs for my clients, all internal and external efforts are connected to the keywords we identify together in our early going. The company's owned and social media channels are used to publish and cross-promote original and earned media content on an ongoing basis, and for analytics, we monitor web traffic, social media statistics, and other business developments in conjunction with our activities. This system tends to deliver solid ROI over time, and activities are always attuned to objectives.

Internal Events

When it comes to public perceptions of a company, it is natural to think of the reputation it has earned with its customers based on its products, services, and the results of its commitments to Customer Experience (CX). But when we think of some of the world's most renowned companies – including those appearing atop the YouGov Brand Index (like Amazon, Google, Netflix, YouTube) – a cult-like mystique comes to mind, based on a meaningful bond or unity perceived among its employees. By and large, this is an attribute of astute leadership and management. In the day-to-day business trenches, leaders of successful companies understand that internal meetings represent vital steps in celebrating and advancing a company's culture. Therefore, even though meetings are not always viewed as being productive, for well-run companies, each one is a very real opportunity to engage, enrich, and motivate employees individually, and to fortify invaluable cultural bonds across groups.

- Read this story from ITA Group to learn more about transforming a company's culture through internal events: http://bit.ly/2uqa3mC.

The creators of event marketing platform GEVME have published a quality list of the most common types of corporate events. The internal ones, primarily intended for employees but often featuring VIP guests or entertainers, include appreciation events; board meetings; business dinners; holiday parties; incentive trips; training and team-building affairs.[18]

Since these can often be wrangled by simple emails, physical invitations or word-of-mouth, I am covering them first. Across the spectrum from board meetings to holiday parties, the emotional possibilities for attendees run the gamut. Still, each of these initiative types is subject to failure or success depending upon the communications support they receive. From our toolset, you will want to clarify objectives with the executives driving the event beforehand, use the copy platform to establish the guiding parameters for the event and your promotions, and then apply strategic campaign thinking, using direct messaging – as well as the company's owned and social media channels, as relevant, depending upon the event specifics.

In keeping with the importance of integrating PR activities with overall marketing, it is also well worth establishing measures for ROI assessment. For example, surveying attendees beforehand and/or afterward may improve gatherings and introduce unforeseen efficiencies.

In short, your efforts to bring this constructive mindset to bear on internal events can identify essential ingredients for follow-up communications activities (newsletters, recognition programs, annual reports, recruitment language, etc.). Normally, talent retention and profitability, as well as the maintenance of strong culture, are mission essential company objectives: Therefore, the diligent and enthusiastic application of your skill set in the service of internal events is sure to make you an MVP.

External Events

Dovetailing into corporate events that go beyond employees, I want to share another great story summarizing event types. Ronnie Higgins published this feature for Eventbrite in 2018: "6 Types of Corporate Events (and How to Make Them Fun)," http://bit.ly/2FVnVN6.[19] Comparing Mr. Higgins' list with the one from GEVME, here is a rundown of external corporate event types: awards events; conferences, festivals, and trade shows; charity events; product launches; seminars and workshops.

While the communications consultant's organizational approach to maximizing the value of external events mostly follows the same path prescribed for internal ones, there is one big difference: Informing the constituents or invitees is a much more strategic and large-scale affair.

For this fruitful realm of business, the impacts of trends in digitalization and mobility are driving innovation in apps and software that provide highly intelligent solutions. One company, Bizzabo, refers to its offering as the world's number one rated event software[20] – and the company's content marketing certainly qualifies it as a youtility. In this resourceful story, the company qualifies its expertise by painstakingly guiding readers through the process of organizing their event strategy: https://blog.bizzabo.com/event-strategy.[21]

Across the board, DWA's clientele regularly engage in certain industry events. The most common ones are awards shows, which often are presented as part of a conference, and may include trade shows (with booths), and several days' worth of keynote presentations, breakout sessions, workshops, and cocktail receptions. Although submitting a project for award consideration, and then purchasing tickets to attend the conference, are easy ways to gain official access to the festivities, it is not uncommon for both up-and-coming and well-established entrepreneurs to sneak in. When one's competitors and desired clients all gather in one place, the fear of missing out (FOMO) is strong enough to drive desperate measures to be included. Even that haphazard framework warrants a sound strategy: Bizzabo's in-depth guide can take the planning process, and the desired results, to another level.

Trade show exhibition, presenting speeches, hosting workshops, sponsoring award shows and receptions, and even launching and promoting original conferences and workshops from start to finish; for the past several years, my agenda has constantly involved me in supporting initiatives like these. Given the importance of large-scale events to my clients and their clients, I have chosen to regularly communicate about them as one of my agency's content marketing calling cards. By promoting Ultimate Events – a carefully curated list that features film and music festivals, business gatherings, and other events likely to be of interest to my target audiences – there are countless benefits for myself and my business. Those advantages serve me well in helping other companies maximize their investments into external events.

Bizzabo's guidance leads from planning to launching, promoting, managing, and wrapping up any given event, in strategic fashion. As with internal events, it may be on you to clarify objectives with leaders, use the copy platform to hone-in on guiding communications parameters, and then apply strategic campaign thinking to engage target audiences and drive the desired results. Whether it is all on you or you are part of a team, from the registration phase through the event itself and afterward, your corporate communications contributions are sure to be of critical importance.

According to Social Coup's CEO Julius Solaris, there is a takeaway from recent research on event apps that I find fascinating: the sections for Sessions, Engagement and Attendee Profiles reportedly get the most use, with sections for Sponsors and Ticketing being used the least.[22] You can learn more about the Bizzabo app and all its features here: https://www.bizzabo.com/event-app.

Specifically, from the PR angle, I look at event participation as having three phases: Before, during and after. If you are serving as the event organizer, it is on you to lead the communications strategy, to have your campaign planned out and fired up for all three phases, and to empower all participants (speakers, sponsors, vendors, etc.) to be able to promote their involvement and contribute to your overall objectives. The approaches involve pursuing earned media, engaging in content marketing and ideally some branded content initiatives ... all of which ramps up to drive registrations and other key performance indicators.

Media Relations for External Events

A special consideration for external events is that when they are successfully packaged and promoted, members of the media will be interested in attending. Providing complimentary credentials allowing free access to working press is expected, but also, it is a policy that needs to be extremely well thought out and managed. While having media attend and cover an event is very desirable, attendance does not guarantee coverage. Therefore, the need to encourage coverage in exchange for each granted credential is very real.

As one example of how a large organization addresses this, the administrators of SXSW require an application process that includes a Letter of Assignment from a media outlet to validate the fact that the applying journalist will be worth admitting. For SXSW, there is also a 15-business-day lead time on the granting of press credentials.

While the need for governing press credential provision is clear from the organizers' point-of-view, even reasonable gatekeeping can backfire when it comes to the media. SXSW learned this a decade ago, when a columnist for TechNewsWorld was denied a pass, and used his platform to complain.[23] Yes, the field of media members is growing, with the proliferation of blogs and podcasts, and accommodating the needs of all concerned stands to be a very tall order. Still, the most deftly run event press offices take all of this into account. There is usually a press room of some sort, which acts as a communications clearinghouse for news releases and media alerts coming out of the event and provides places for journalists to roost and do their work. If they have special requests for interviews with keynote speakers or other executives involved in the show, the press room staff members will do their best to help coordinate.

Support for attending press continues after the show wraps, promoting earned media coverage, and extending strategic communications activities to support any objectives left standing … for example, paving the way for the next edition of the event by promoting its date and location.

Comparing the challenges of operating an entire press office for a large-scale event to supporting a single event speaker – or even just a smaller event, like a press conference – the before-during-after framework still applies. Referring to the super-important media luminaries I exist to serve on behalf of my clients, these situations also demand diplomacy, diligence, professionalism, and patience in the supporting role … followed by proactive promotional excellence when results appear.

Throughout my career, I have embraced the idea that failing to plan is essentially planning to fail. Especially regarding a company's involvement in large-scale events, a great deal of luck would be required to produce success without devising goals and employing strategies to achieve desirable results. Becoming an accomplished communications consultant – a PR Champion, in the words of Deirdre Breakenridge – will require you to master everything discussed and alluded to in this chapter. This book helps you plan. With the desire to develop invaluable superpowers capable of converting failure into success, and a commitment to lifelong learning, your potential for achievement is unlimited.

Exploration

1. You are asked to write two stories today, but you only have time to write one. How do you choose?
2. Name five ways that PR results can be measured.
3. Imagine a small business where the owner has committed to engaging a PR consultant. If the effect of PR activities on organizational performance is important, how can that be measured?
4. Changing attitudes, perceptions, and beliefs is a goal of integrated marketing. How is the practice of social media listening related to this?
5. Name five examples of activities among business executives that might attract negative attention from breaking news journalists?
6. What is the value of 15 media contacts you have found and validated as being relevant for a client through your own diligence, compared with a list of 100 contacts provided by that client's former publicist?
7. List five reasons why using a telephone is likely to be essential in placing a story in the media?

8. Author a pitch inviting journalists to attend a VIP event being staged by your client where original research will be presented, and then find a friendly journalist you can run it past to see if it is something that would interest them, if it was real. Ask your contact if making the invitation exclusive would impact their interest.
9. Attend a meet-up or other local event of your choosing and evaluate its merits by scoring these organizational aspects on a scale of 1 to 5, 5 being the highest: Communications; Leadership; Engagement; Results. For each aspect, suggest a means for improving its merits.
10. For the event you attended for question 9, try to help line up a media interview for one of the organizers, or do the interview yourself.
11. Once the question 10 interview occurs, use your owned and social media channels – and those of the underlying group or organization – to promote it far and wide. Also plan and execute a second promotional phase several weeks after the first round.
12. Measure and summarize the results of the question 11 campaign effort.
13. Now, use your insights gained through the question 9–12 activities to plan a branded content initiative, and execute it across the metaverse used for question 11.
14. Measure the results of your branded content initiative and compile a case study summarizing your work on this account. Plan and execute a promotional campaign to share this case study on your metaverse.
15. If you had the opportunity to perform these types of activities for any leader, company, non-profit or issue in the world, what would you choose, and why? Write an essay laying out your choice(s), identifying the "home runs" you would aim to hit and specifying the other objectives you would hope to fulfill. For extra credit, reach out to the person or organization and share your dream with them. Can you imagine how powerful this story will be if you can make your dream come true?

Notes

1 Borchers, M. (2014, May 26). Measuring the ROI of Public Relations: Five Experts Weigh In. HuffPost. http://bit.ly/PR_ROI
2 Clark, D. (2017, September 26). Myth: PR Campaigns Can't Be Measured. SmartBug Media. http://bit.ly/PR_track
3 Wikipedia contributors. (2020, September 27). Barcelona Principles. Wikipedia. https://en.wikipedia.org/wiki/Barcelona_Principles
4 Simpson, C. (1998). The Day We Closed the News Bureau. *CASE Currents Magazine*. Published.

5. Darnell, R. (2021, May 25). Media View Spectrum [Illustration]. Darnell Works. https://www.darnellworks.com
6. Patel, N. (2019, March 7). Marketing Insider: 5 Rules to Make or Break Influencer Marketing Results. MediaPost. http://bit.ly/2Up2bOL
7. How to Get TechCrunch to Cover Your Startup. (2019, October 16). Quora. http://bit.ly/TCcovet
8. The Air Force Departmental Publishing Office (AFDPO). (2011, January 24). Inverted Pyramid [Illustration]. Wikipedia. http://bit.ly/INVpyr
9. Stewart, J. (2017, July 27). How to Publicize a Garden Walk and Other Local Events. The Publicity Hound. http://ow.ly/pOhH30dHOuv
10. Etchison, R. (2020, May 10). How to Pitch Media Exclusives in Tech PR. Crenshaw Communications. http://bit.ly/PRtheOne
11. American Speech-Language-Hearing Association. (n.d.). Tips for Media Interviews. Retrieved May 17, 2021, from https://www.asha.org/Articles/Tips-for-Media-Interviews/
12. Walker, T. J. (2011, August 19). The Art of the Sound Bite - Media Training. Forbes. http://bit.ly/S_Bite
13. O'Brien, M. (2011). A Website That Works: How Marketing Agencies Can Create Business Generating Sites. RockBench Publishing.
14. Baer, J. (2013). Youtility: Why Smart Marketing Is About Help Not Hype (Illustrated ed.). Portfolio.
15. Legorburu, G., & McColl, D. (2014). Storyscaping: Stop Creating Ads, Start Creating Worlds (1st ed.). Wiley.
16. Lopes, M. (2017, September 15). What is Branded Content? The DVI Group. http://bit.ly/2FLz8Ph
17. Shackelford, J. (2018). Q & A with Lauren Lawson-Zilai. PRSA Content Connection. Published.
18. Tomakh, A. (2021, February 10). The Top 10 Most Common Types of Corporate Events. GEVME. http://bit.ly/2K2kA31
19. Higgins, R. (2018, November 7). 6 Types of Corporate Events (and How to Make Them Fun). Eventbrite US Blog. http://bit.ly/2FVnVN6
20. Wagner, C. (2019, February 5). Event Apps: The Complete List. EventMB. http://bit.ly/EVapp19
21. Bizzabo. (2019, November 12). Event Strategy: The 2020 Guide. https://blog.bizzabo.com/event-strategy
22. Solaris, J. (2019, April 12). Julius Solaris on Twitter. http://bit.ly/2Z2G5Es
23. San Miguel, R. (2010, February 26). A Sour-Grapes Special: SXSW Snubs. TechNewsWorld. http://bit.ly/SXsour

5
Advanced Communications and Marketing Strategies and Tactics

Every day, there are communications feats being achieved at higher levels. In every awards program, those who claim the grand prizes rise above all others involved, if only for a moment. Take heart in this: With perseverance and a little luck, as your career progresses and your expertise grows, it is likely you will work yourself to the top of your industry. When you do, the opportunities will elevate.

To me, those who work in investor relations operate in the realm of advanced communications and marketing strategies every day. A specific example of success in that province played out in early 2019. At a time when the world's largest brands were collectively altering their marketing approaches, resulting in drastic changes in how they work with ad agencies, Procter & Gamble's Chief Brand Officer Marc Pritchard hit the road hard, with an explicit goal: In highly publicized speeches at industry events and in follow-up interviews, he touted P&G's "new media supply chain" as something that all marketers should embrace. The response from investors drove P&G's stock price to a new high.[1]

Think about this: What would the financial impact of such strategic moves be if there were no media outlets to report Mr. Pritchard's talking points?

As a publicly traded company, P&G is compelled to increase its value for shareholders; that objective is a constant motivation for executives and employees alike. Commanding over U.S. $70 billion in 2020 revenue,[2] P&G's directors naturally have a distinct view of the world compared with most other business executives. The company is of wide interest to the business community at-large, and to investors. Therefore, its ability to command attention is beyond question, which firmly establishes it on a higher plane. Up there, the potential rewards are colossal … but what about the risks?

While P&G's campaign was gaining steam, the leaders behind the merger of consumer packaged goods giants Kraft and Heinz reported a write-off exceeding U.S. $15 billion, while also revealing that the SEC was investigating the

DOI: 10.4324/9781003177913-8

underlying business practices ... all of which led to a massive drop in stock prices.[3] Personally, I would have considered myself very lucky to have been invited to support the teams behind this massive business development at 3G, Berkshire Hathaway, Kraft or Heinz, but seeing this milepost on their journey certainly gives pause. Had my counsel been requested, would I have sensed the trouble ahead, and been able to steer clear?

These are important concerns to take to heart before cracking open the following playbook for your clients. Essentially, unless you and your client embrace "failing fast" and you are fully prepared for fallout, attempting to wield advanced strategies and tactics is unlikely to produce positive, sustainable, long-term results. Validation of this premise abounds in a 2001 article from business visionary Jim Collins summarizing his book, "Good to Great: Why Some Companies Make the Leap ... And Others Don't."[4] In the previous chapter, we concluded that success in the field of communications requires mastery over every subject and discipline we have explored together. To have a reasonable shot at working, advanced tactics need to be built on a solid foundation. At the higher level, missteps can easily sink your ship.

In the pages ahead, we will get more specific about advanced communications and marketing strategies as they relate to generating Returns on Investments (ROI) – including earned media coverage – effectively and consistently. Deciding if the conditions are right for springing into action is entirely up to you.

Sounding Out the Right Strategy

Assuming you ask the right questions, the initial client interview can be expected to illuminate the company's objectives, and the resources its executives might be willing to invest to achieve them. When engaging with a P&G brand, any of the latest YouGov honorees or entertainment empires like HBO, the reputation, leadership, culture, and customer relationships for such "Alphas" are likely to be solid, unlike many smaller companies where you may be the only person with any strength in those areas. Referring to the Project Management Triangle, where work is so often classified as being good, fast, or cheap (pick two), my typical experience is supporting companies that choose to save money, which might translate into meaning good, cheap, and ordinarily, not too fast. Whenever they want to increase the pace of progress, I will help estimate the higher costs, and offer to flex their budget to accommodate their wishes. With a client that is willing to spend, it is especially important to plan for being good and fast. Most leaders expect miraculous marketing on thrifty budgets, so before any initiative begins, I strongly advise taking the time to consider how best to support that scenario, too.

Advanced Strategies and Tactics

Welcome to Tier Two. Knowing that client size can have a far-reaching effect on a communications consultant's role, add in a client's unbridled ambition and ample funding, and our hot-seat position can start to sizzle. To avoid being burned, you must decide if you believe in the company's leadership and its values and proceed accordingly. If you instinctively feel there is a conflict with your personal leadership brand, your best bet may be to seek work elsewhere.

Choosing to proceed, however, your commitment to continuous learning must be solid, as any Tier Two company will be hungry to grow – and therefore, aiming to hire the best and brightest, and expecting everyone to soar. Assuming you are all-in on this client, and willing to risk everything to help it succeed, exploring the following assessments more deeply will lead you to some proven tactics that can reasonably be expected to help win the day, and possibly, the entire war.

For fortifying brand strategy, the POSTAR model is a proven system for moving from research through strategic planning and into action methodically and effectively. Remember to assess and build all plans atop Positioning, Objectives, Strategies and Tactics, manage all these functions together through Administration, and to measure Results. Doing so will firmly establish the basis for every activity and ensure the soundness of your programs.

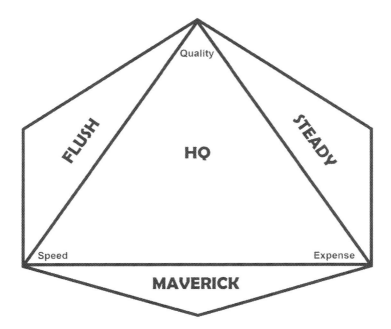

Figure 5: Client Strength Finder[5]
Source: Darnell, R. (2021, May 25). Darnell Works. https://www.darnellworks.com

The High-Quality (HQ) Strategy

It is not hard to imagine having an Alpha client with Tier Two status or ambitions. These companies embrace a High-Quality (HQ) strategy, where there is no compromise among the three "good, fast and cheap" choices. A typical game plan might be expressed like so: *Our company is committed to using advanced marketing tactics in a way that is highly calculated, and to measuring, adjusting, and sustaining our efforts over time.*

To generate the right results, its leaders are perfectly willing to incur costs, they can be patient, and expectations for work quality are high. Especially for companies that fit the HQ description – which are committed to supporting the Continuous Customer Journey by facilitating positive Customer Experiences (CX); embrace design thinking and creative innovation; seek to leverage mobility and digitalization intelligently; and lead by example – certain activities have higher affinity.

Charged with building an advanced communications program to support this strategy, consider these tactics we will discuss further in the next section.

Table 3: Strong Suits for HQ Strategy

Advanced Tactic #	Description	Consider
1	Content Marketing	Requires expertise, diligence, commitment
2	Media Relations	Requires expertise, diligence, commitment
3	Interviews	Requires expertise, diligence, commitment
4	Analyst and Influencer Relations	Requires diplomacy, diligence, commitment
10	Promotions and Promo Items	Brand elements and values in action
11	Guerilla Marketing, including Experiential	Make the right impressions in the right ways
12	Advertising and Direct Marketing	Surprise, delight, connect, authentically
13	Trade Shows	Tactics alter widely based on budget
14	Award Shows	Tactics alter widely based on budget

The Steady Strategy

In my view, the fact that I do not live in a major market provides some very practical benefits. If my office had a Times Square address, I might have a harder time connecting with clients who share my preferences for methodical strategies and tactics driven by patience and practicality. Many of my favorite entrepreneurs focus first on being good and cost-effective, while readily acknowledging the downside of moving too fast. Most would endorse this type of strategy: *Our company is interested in achieving success that is sustainable using marketing tactics that are smart, cost-effective, and manageable.*

These leaders seek to achieve success using means that are reliable, preferring to plan actions thoroughly and to make sound financial decisions over riskier ones, even when that means missing momentous opportunities. Being innovative is appealing, but only when chances for above-average returns can be substantiated.

Steady companies are essentially like HQ ones, just more financially conservative. It therefore follows that they either stand on solid leadership ground, or they aspire to. So, surveying the leaders on the perceived importance of foundational ideas like the Continuous Customer Journey, design thinking, creative innovation, mobility, digitalization, leadership, company culture, and values should be instructive. Depending upon your client's priorities in these areas, consider the following.

Table 4: Strong Suits for Steady Strategy

Advanced Tactic #	Description	Consider
1	Content Marketing	Requires expertise, diligence, commitment
7	Client Presentations	Requires time, diligence, and deep focus
8	Books	Time-intensive; far-reaching benefits
9	Speaking Opportunities	Time-intensive; far-reaching benefits
10	Promotions and Promo Items	Brand elements and values in action
11	Guerilla Marketing, including Experiential	Make the right impressions in the right ways
12	Advertising and Direct Marketing	Surprise, delight, connect, authentically
13	Trade Shows	Tactics alter widely based on budget
14	Award Shows	Tactics alter widely based on budget

The Flush Strategy

As part of The Terpin Group, one of the accounts I helped pitch and win in 2000 really stood out. The leaders of this venture, and the board members, all had first-class educations, backgrounds, and connections, and they were on a serious roll. Having closed a U.S. $4.5 million round of financing early in 2000, they would go on to raise millions more. Their branding and promotional marketing efforts targeting the film industry at-large blanketed the Sundance and Cannes Film Festivals that year, as well as other large film markets. Fast forward two years ... at which point their doors closed for good.

My time serving that group was short-lived, and in 2000, I had no idea how things would play out. Still, I had misgivings. Personally, I have never been in the position to spend money freely; if it is not abundantly clear already, I am instinctively thrifty, out of necessity. Nonetheless, there are highly respectable outfits that are in the position to spend lavishly, in a framework that also accommodates quality work and fast-paced activity. NASA's Mars Exploration Program is an excellent federal example; last year's top professional sports franchises probably have similar approaches this year; and, in the world of commerce, rising direct-to-consumer brands like Stitch Fix and Harry's appear to fit that bill.[6] Summarizing their marketing strategy might look like this: *Achieving our ambitious goals for growth and profitability requires us to lead our market, which harnesses aggressive marketing to outpace our competitors.*

Leaders in such ventures are bound to be ultra-competitive and hawkish. When funds are available to advance any good prospect for increased success, and when the desire to win is constant, the Fear of Missing Out (FOMO) can lead to behavior that resembles an erupting volcano. Charged with building an advanced communications program to support this strategy, consider the following (Table 5).

The Maverick Strategy

The last possibility of the "pick two" triangle presents a company that prioritizes moving quickly on a tight budget. Such a group will represent a challenge for even the most astute practitioner, since few leaders are going to freely admit to a corporate disregard for quality. Maybe your initial briefing will uncover sentiments like a willingness to fail fast, or the need

Table 5: Strong Suits for Flush Strategy

Advanced Tactic #	Description	Consider
1	Content Marketing	Requires expertise, diligence, commitment
5	Original Blogs, Videos, Podcasts, Apps	Can be built relatively quickly
6	Original Events	Can be built relatively quickly
10	Promotions and Promo Items	Brand elements and values in action
11	Guerilla Marketing, including Experiential	Make the right impressions in the right ways
12	Advertising and Direct Marketing	Surprise, delight, connect, authentically
13	Trade Shows	Tactics alter widely based on budget
14	Award Shows	Tactics alter widely based on budget

to stake a claim quickly, perhaps acknowledging that the more sensible planning efforts will come into effect later, when conditions improve. You may hear, "for now, we just need to get it done," with little more to go on. The more politically correct version may sound like this: *Our company is interested in using advanced marketing tactics cost-effectively to achieve certain results ASAP.*

Given all my forewarnings, my counsel that such a ship is probably sinking will come as no surprise. To be perfectly clear, in my experience, such a challenge should be considered very high-risk. Nonetheless, you may have no choice but to proceed. Further, from a more optimistic perspective, there are plenty of stories from the business world of successful turnarounds, where intelligently applying this Maverick strategy proved effective. Charged with building an advanced communications program to support one, consider the following (Table 6).

80   PR Client Services

Table 6: Strong Suits for Maverick Strategy

Advanced Tactic #	Description	Consider
1	Content Marketing	Requires expertise, diligence, commitment
10	Promotions and Promo Items	Brand elements and values in action
11	Guerilla Marketing, including Experiential	Make the right impressions in the right ways
12	Advertising and Direct Marketing	Surprise, delight, connect, authentically
13	Trade Shows	Tactics alter widely based on budget
14	Award Shows	Tactics alter widely based on budget

Advanced Tactics

This set of high-level communications activities covers everything I have ever done for a client, once we established our platform. The high volume of forewarnings and emphasis on strategic assessments is provided to ensure you take proper aim before firing away in any of the following directions.

Before proceeding, let's reflect for one more moment.

You probably noticed that the word "cheap" has been used liberally in this chapter, interchangeably with synonyms like thrifty and cost-effective. In these pages, defining costs comparatively is constructive, while speaking of them in the workplace is often considered taboo. If you have the good fortune of being hired in a communications capacity, and if your client is asking you to help maximize investments of any size as they apply to activities like the following, aim high and go with confidence. This listing is sorted according to my sense of the requisite complexity and sophistication of each endeavor. Fueled with the power to innovate, every tactic listed here is subject to being hacked for spectacular results.

1. Content Marketing (especially fitting for HQs, but applicable to all)
   Remember the discussions about being a Youtility, where a pool installation company builds its success by using its owned and social media channels to educate consumers on swimming pools? Day-to-day and

month-to-month, behavioral trends are subject to massive swings. Account for new findings – as well as the well-known and the familiar, like seasons and holidays – in presenting informative subject matter that is told from the POV of the brand, its leaders, and or those who exemplify the company at its best. Level up: Remember to engage audiences in these activities, to demonstrate your commitment to CX and relate your story through the eyes of the customers.

2. Media Relations (especially fitting for HQs)

   By committing to a media-relations strategy, any organization demonstrates its active engagement in the world of professional communications. Consistently issuing meaningful news releases, generating earned media coverage around business developments, and aiming to have a company's name, its leaders and its accomplishments warrant attention, the impact on trustworthiness and perceived efficacy can be monumental. Level up: Handling media relationships with great care and tending them to last over time is imperative. Sound use of exclusives – and consideration of paid engagement with branded content labs inside major media outlets, like The New York Times' T Brand Studio – can produce dream-worthy results.

3. Interviews (especially fitting for HQs)

   Being invited to be interviewed by any media outlet is usually an advanced tactic, since getting others to take interest in what an executive has to say often requires diligence. Understanding that most reporters want dirt, media interest (in the form of questions) can put interview subjects on defense. This is where leadership, values, missions, and objectives provide the foundation. In his time, Bob Hope was a larger-than-life media icon. Media coaches and luminaries champion the public speaking traits he embodied so elegantly, always adjusting his message to his audience, using uplifting humor to engage personally, and imparting stories or anecdotes sure to be relevant, and likely to be inspirational. Level up: Take the offensive strategically. Research the interviewer, prepare and rehearse talking points, and demonstrate appreciation for the opportunity by being warm, genuine, and thoughtful. Give listeners something to think about or act upon through your commentary.

4. Analyst and Influencer Relations (especially fitting for HQs)

   While media interviews expose company leaders directly to audiences, the goals of building relationships with analysts and influencers are meant to be even more impactful. Essentially, you hope to educate them on your products and/or services, so that you can access their intelligence and gain their feedback, for use in improving the company's offerings. When all goes well, these qualified experts will use their platforms to promote your firm. There is a considerable cost involved in attaining the benefits – and a great number of risks as well, should your products, services or communications efforts fall short of expectations. Level up: Research is the key to setting sights properly, identifying and avoiding pitfalls, and underwriting the potential of successful analyst and influencer collaborations. To increase the positive prospects, ensure your team exercises diligence in problem finding – and problem solving – prior to engaging with analysts and influencers.

5. Original Blogs, Videos, Podcasts, and Apps (especially fitting for the Flush)
Building reputation, positioning a company, inspiring action, attracting prospects, completing sales; achieving any of these objectives requires a business to attract attention. A good website will leverage the strengths of demonstrating a company's value to customers and the commitment to solving their problems, using storytelling. A blog, a video series, and/or a podcast is a bold means for telling the world you have something to say. Level up: Make a plan that ensures your focused communications initiatives are strategically sound, topical, and reflect the brand, its positioning, and its overall mission (or, a specific part of its mission) over time.

6. Original Events (especially fitting for the Flush)
Chapter 4 sums up the important details of both internal and external corporate events. These represent extremely rich opportunities to build and fortify living, breathing connections with VIPs. Level up: Create an event that addresses the most important marketing objectives your client is facing. Begin with the organizing idea, plan and activate "Before, During and After" communications at the right times, and create content dedicated to providing information on and about your event that is up-to-date and easy for constituents to find.

7. Client Presentations (especially fitting for the Steady)
In the business-to-business (B2B) world, the need to connect with prospects to present capabilities is existential. Today's elevated sales strategy is brought to life with smart content marketing, where success can result in partnering, collaboration, and the delivery of effective solutions. What does it look like to excel in a B2B client presentation? Imagine using your limited time so effectively that your prospects gain a full understanding of exactly what it is like to work with you. Level up: Through the advanced development and use of case studies, this goal is achievable. Visit https://www.winwithoutpitching.com/case-studies for more details. For the consumer-driven business, adopt the same mindset: Use all reasonable means to consistently and professionally demonstrate to your potential customers how your company works to deliver value, and to generate positive experiences.

8. Books, White Papers, and Studies (especially fitting for the Steady)
   For an initiative where a communications consultant can provide vital support, where a company and its leaders can level-up and expect to make a long-lasting impact, I recommend the development of original books, white papers, and/or studies. While not a fit for every situation, and the commitments required are extraordinarily deep, stepping into initiatives like this put a leader on a path that is exceptionally rewarding, from research and storytelling perspectives, and many others. As emphasized throughout these pages, there is great power in stories and in their telling. The trailer for the book "The Storytelling Edge" from the principals of Contently makes these points very effectively, as you can see here: http://bit.ly/TrailerTSE. While Contently has been successful as a company, think about all the marketing opportunities that were activated when the principals brought out their new book – and stories from it, and stories about it – in their business developments.
9. Public Speaking (especially fitting for the Steady)
   Proving that you have a message that is worthy of people's attention is highly compelling. Drawing them in, leaving them with a laugh or some tale that endears them to you is so ambitious that many people focus a great deal of energy on their fear of public speaking. Level up: Learn the basics from experts like Lars Sudmann (http://bit.ly/LarsCODE), who encourages us all to get out there, focusing on Content, Organization, Delivery and Effect (CODE) to bring leadership to life.[7] By starting small but persisting, the willingness to pursue and embrace these opportunities can blossom and grow into other realms, where a brand's mission, values and objectives can align, activate and soar (for example, investor relations).
   For all these tactics, I have flagged them to indicate their fits with HQ, Flush, and/or Steady strategies. That does not mean a group favoring a Steady approach should not consider content media relations or interviews: They should. Since this chapter is dedicated to identifying advanced tactics with strong strategic alignment, activities are being prioritized based on expected fit. Each of the following tactics was listed as being relevant for Mavericks. In any situation where a client is seeking to make an impact, any of these have proven effectiveness, especially when built upon a solid marketing platform.
10. Promotions and Promo Items
    In the same ways that an organizing idea can be used to maximize the results of creating an original event, that same unifying theme forms a smart basis for devising the use of promotions and promotional items. These two tactics are distinct from one another: The first might represent

a sale, a contest, or a connection to an event (back to school sale, find the golden ticket); the latter can be any item featuring a company's name, logo, or mascot, like a pen or a luggage tag. Level up: Think about the behavior and actions you want to inspire among your customers and use this marketing expenditure to influence them accordingly. Let the golden ticket inspire ideas for groundbreaking promotions. My favorite example of a promo item is the Staples Easy Button; people pay good money for this tchotchke which promotes an office supply store with a hopeful message that is otherwise useless.

11. Guerilla Marketing, including Experiential

    These tactics tend to play out on the streets, in high-traffic areas where crowds can be engaged, and targeted actions achieved. In the introduction of Scion, ATTIK used many such activations to creatively circumvent the known aversion of their youthful audience to marketing. These days, using exciting new technologies to wow fans and make impressions, experiential campaigns (which I view as outgrowths of guerilla marketing, although they are typically paid for and legitimized through permitting, etc.) are growing in scale, intensity, and excitement. Level up: With so many ways to reach audiences, figuring out how to bring engagement to life across different media platforms – and in real life – can be incredibly inspiring, as evidenced at theme parks every day. The ideal tactic in this category escalates positive associations with the entity behind the scenes, so make sure the stunts are memorable for all the right reasons.

12. Advertising and Direct Marketing

    A staple of the marketing plan for so many brands, advertising is tried-and-true for some, and a monumental failure for others. AMC's original series "The Pitch" provided a fascinating record of advertising industry experts attempting to win major accounts. To me, those exercises clearly identified the infinite challenges to marketing effectiveness, in the form of all-knowing clients, haphazard business relationships, impossible timelines and inadequate research. Direct marketing uses email, mail, and the telephone to deliver messaging straight to the intended audiences. Level up: Reverse engineer your recipe for success from other campaigns that have demonstrated effectiveness. There is an award for this ultimate of measures, called the Effie Awards. In 2019, "It's a Tide Ad" won P&G the Grand Effie, earning acclaim for its strategy and its creativity. With an eye toward what has worked for others who advertise, and why it worked for them, focus in on the brand, its value to customers and the authentic manifestations occurring in those interactions. History shows that the short stories told in ads can set brands apart from their competition for years to come.

13. Trade Shows – Sponsoring, Exhibiting, Attending, Hacking
    Taking an active role in a trade show is not for the faint of heart. When a company's competitors congregate to present polished versions of themselves, celebrate their combined achievements and collectively take aim for the future, the lowest level of participation is attendance. From there, the rungs succeed upward (each requiring higher costs) to exhibiting and sponsorship. Many will sneak in, jump the lines, violate the promotional guidelines and/or otherwise attempt to barnstorm and steal attention. Some of my favorite examples of successful trade show strategy involve playing by the rules, but still seeking opportunities to captivate. Level up: Just as an ad is going to be judged based on how and where it is delivered, corporate participation in a trade show is going to be constrained by the identity and governance of the show. How can your brand best leverage that platform? Should you lead, follow, amplify the theme in an unforgettable way?
14. Award Shows – Sponsoring, Exhibiting, Submitting, Attending, Hacking
    Here we find yet another widely acknowledged means for substantiating success, which many non-conformists cynically dismiss as being elitist and insulated. Admittedly, the submission fees for most are exorbitant, and those funds will yield zero returns if every single step of the award show involvement is not treated with extreme care and thoughtfulness. Level up: Crystallize your plans around your objectives and ensure the best and brightest from the client company are involved in preparing any/all awards submissions. If it is the intern or someone with little industry experience filling out the forms, do not be surprised if the honors fail to materialize. Award shows happen at a moment in time, and certain things happen before, during and immediately afterward. Communicating about a win is expected; think about going further, to shine the light on the clients, the workers behind the scenes, and even what the turn of events means for the winner's customers.

Exploration

1. From the description of Marc Pritchard's successful campaign aimed at bolstering P&G's bottom line, list the communications tactics he used. Which of the four strategies do you feel P&G fits into, and how many communications professionals do you think are involved behind-the-scenes for the company?
2. In the article "Fast, Good or Cheap. Pick Three?" (http://bit.ly/fgcp3) the author takes issue with the project management triangle.[8] Invoking "Brooks' Law," he relates it to the idiom stating too many cooks spoil

the broth. Based on the situation described with the Kraft/Heinz merger, what are your thoughts on what might have gone wrong?
3. You meet a potential new client who tells you money is no object, and they want a story on the front page of a certain newspaper ASAP. Where do you start?
4. You have an opportunity to lead communications for a non-profit for a funding drive. Their fee is minimal. What strategy do they fit into, and what tactics would you consider using?
5. Read this article from Sunnie Giles about failing fast or do your own research on the concept: http://bit.ly/FastFail. List three reasons why failing fast can be a good idea for organizations.
6. You surmise that your client fits the HQ strategy, and they want to bring more attention to their mission. List three tactics that may be relevant and explain how you would proceed in determining the best course of action.
7. You surmise that your client fits the Steady strategy, and it is clear the leaders want to land new clients. List three tactics that may be relevant and explain how you would proceed in determining the best course of action.
8. You surmise that your client fits the Flush strategy, and it is clear the leaders want to "own" an upcoming trade show. Explain how you would proceed in determining the best course of action.
9. You surmise that your client fits the Maverick strategy, and it is clear the leaders want to "crash" an upcoming award show. Explain how you would proceed in determining the best course of action.
10. Explain from your perspective three characteristics of a strong interview prospect. For a journalist, what might be the pros and cons for interviewing a CEO that is driving HQ, Steady, Flush, and Maverick strategies, respectively?

Notes

1 Lash, E. (2019, July 30). P&G Looks Expensive. Morningstar, Inc. http://bit.ly/PGlooks19
2 Procter & Gamble (PG). (n.d.). Forbes. Retrieved May 23, 2021, from https://www.forbes.com/companies/procter-gamble/
3 Coffee, P., & Pearl, D. (2019, March 27). Was the 3G Kraft Heinz Mega-Merger Destined to Fail? Adweek. http://adweek.it/2TFYYcc
4 Collins, Jim, "Good to Great," Fast Company, Oct., 2001. http://bit.ly/2bgreat
5 Illustration: Client Strength Finder, Darnell Works, Inc.

6 Mahoney, S. (2019, June 10). D2C FYI: Secret To D2C Brands' Allure? Outspending Everyone Else. MediaPost. http://bit.ly/D2Cspend
7 TEDxFlanders – Lars Sudmann – On public speaking. (2010, September 22). [Video]. YouTube. https://youtu.be/AdRuBRR6xOU
8 business.com. (2020, April 14). Fast, Good or Cheap – Pick Three? http://bit.ly/fgcp3

Part II
Agency Business

Topics Covered

Agency Management   91
Professional Development   108
Scaling and Exit Strategies and Tactics   119

6
Agency Management

Many businesses have extremely humble origins, and I have had the pleasure of supporting a lot of great ones that started out very simply. Two design school students in England decided to start a company and used a grandparent's unused attic for space (ATTIK). Asked to bid on a job soon after going freelance, another designer used her last name for her new corporation (Sarofsky). And this PR professional, upon leaving an established LA firm, chose The Darnell Works Agency as the d.b.a. ("Doing Business As") name for a new venture with its own roster of clients.

Whereas ATTIK's founders had little to start with when they conceived their business – until earning a grant from The Prince's Trust – Erin Sarofsky had a potential client lined up … and I started DWA with a couple of clients onboard. The nuts and bolts of starting a business (name, logo, business card, email address, phone number, and bank account) were essential in each of our early goings. In each case, there also was some need to position ourselves, but much of that was done on-the-fly, through personal interactions, tenacity, and deeds, where the vital essence of the deal was showing up, getting to work, and proving ourselves.

Over time, ATTIK became world famous in the design community for its ethos, as well as its work … where branding was enshrined, design was worshiped, and youth audiences were prioritized. Sarofsky's special sauce is also catalyzed by design, plus many other factors which have arisen organically through perseverance, to set its reputation and internal culture apart. Having focused on PR for emerging high-tech businesses at The Terpin Group, I gladly homed-in on the creative industry as my realm of specialization.

Expanding a business operation from freelancing to forging a reputable brand is not something every independent contractor accomplishes, and I

DOI: 10.4324/9781003177913-10

am grateful for the real-world education I have received on the importance of brand building: I consider this to be a secret of my success.

The founders of Leviathan had a slightly different origination story. Three men united a little further along in their careers, after the principal had ended another frustrating partnership. His new allies were eager to embrace fresh challenges for their talents and ambitions. When the venture launched, its business plan was well formed, and while some of the early work was outside its targeted niche, within a few years, Leviathan had earned its place atop the field of experiential design.

Anyone surveying the world of public relations and communications will quickly surmise that the space is densely populated; still, depending upon the clients' needs and particulars, finding a great fit might be difficult. The J.R. O'Dwyer Company is a New York-based publisher covering PR and marketing communications that consistently ranks the top U.S. PR firms, as you can see here: http://bit.ly/UStopPR. Look at all those firms, all that revenue, all those full-time employees ready to serve the communications needs of entrepreneurs!

From the top of O'Dwyer's list, you can also search by region or by specialty. According to conventional thinking, if a communications business is ever going to be worthy of attracting the best of the best, it would probably need to appear on that list, cross-referenced by location and specialty, right? Let's digress for a moment. Over the course of this journey, you are expanding your expertise in this field, and using that to engage with businesspeople that can benefit from your knowledge and diligence. Now, consider that on odwyerpr.com, you will not find my business listed, nor will you find any of the firms or consultancies I consider to be my main competitors.

As the principal of a business that has stood the test of time, which consistently delivers excellent value to its clientele and rewards me generously, I am incredibly proud. Clearly, you do not need to be at the very top of any niche to have job security or to achieve success as a communications consultant. With that said, there are certain hallmarks of business success – most of which probably abound among those appearing in O'Dwyer's listings – that can elevate your operation, if you are smart, motivated, and disciplined.

The Arena

Each of the topics I refer to as comprising the bedrock tenets of business success is intricately connected to the inner workings of my business. To make the case for the importance of reputation management and ethics, creativity, strategy, personal brands, branding and the consulting mindset, let's analyze what happens when I receive a new business inquiry. Such a catalyst triggers a series of well-rehearsed reactions on my part, prompting questions I need answered and research I must complete. In short, these means are necessary to assess my prospect's strengths in each of these core areas, so I can evaluate them against my current standing as an independent provider of services that is subject to being hired. Before long, there is a judgment on my part: How do I feel about the prospect of working for this person, and does it appear to be a good fit?

Obviously, there are times when all of us are willing to work for anyone who agrees to pay our rate. We can only afford to be more selective when we have less time available to sell. These bottom-line decision-making parameters may be fixed, but even in the situation where one leaps into a job that feels precarious, it is especially important to make a record of the decision ... to improve the ability to learn from it.

In fact, I am adamant about documenting business relationships for one's own benefit. If you are adept with email, keeping track of your exchanges is relatively easy. This book's first chapter includes my initial interview "needs analysis" questions; I recommend using a consistent format to name and save documents capturing answers from those sessions, then storing them intelligently for future reference. I also write multi-page journal entries at least once a week, where I usually have a brief entry for each active client, and others I am in-touch with for business purposes. By cross-referencing this documentation, I am always able to study the arc of any given relationship quite effectively, depending upon how much detail I have recorded.

Journaling also allows me to bring the universe of my business under personal control, where my cares, concerns, and values can take center stage. If something is bothering me – especially if it is consistently troublesome over time – this system allows me to acknowledge it, track it, and act accordingly. By my estimation, anything that causes me to lose sleep is a threat to my business and failing to deal with it might prove disastrous. Without journaling, it can be hard to diagnose problems and prescribe the treatments necessary for wellbeing.

Operating a business for a stretch of time where there are no major problems provides an excellent baseline for understanding where vulnerabilities exist. Of course, managing actual problems can also create experiences that, in hindsight, are brilliantly instructive. My long tenured apprenticeship in engaging with businesspeople factors into my snap judgments. If you take the time to use similar diligence in measuring, assessing, and documenting your client-related activities, at the very least, you will have a better understanding of why you handled things as you did. Even though it is always an educated guess, employing this methodology has bolstered my confidence in evaluating the potential fit of a new business relationship. I fully expect it will do the same for you.

Another benefit of this handling is the positive impact it has on my prospects. My constructive, professionally investigative approaches are intended to be educational for all parties. When I get a new business inquiry, here is what follows.

1. If I have bandwidth to add a client – or even if I don't, but I am immediately impressed by the caller and am willing to spend some time offering free advice to help them understand the framework of engaging a PR consultant – I will set up a call.
    i. Completing the initial conversation may lead to a proposal being generated.
    ii. If I decide not to bid on the account, I will provide one or more referrals and invite the prospect to please keep in touch.
2. Otherwise, relatively quickly, I will respond with a message to thank the prospect, explain that my roster is currently full, express the hope of keeping-in-touch, and provide referral(s).

In scenario 1, even if I am not intending to bid on an account in the immediate future, I have learned that change is certain, and probably within a few months, I will need a new client. That insight has prompted me to seize the day and attempt to make a friend whenever my phone rings, even if my roster is completely full and I am super-busy. Those investments of my time have paid dividends: more than once, they have led to client engagements further down the road; perhaps more importantly, the positive result is usually a person who thinks – and is likely to speak – more highly of me.

As you can see, these are situations where ethics are communicated through strategic actions, exponentially benefitting my reputation while aiming to create value for everyone involved.

This new business threshold is one place where every bedrock tenet of business success is incredibly important. By embracing creativity, your personal brand, and your strategy for operating as a professional every day, you will be in the best position to handle your client and prospect relationships regardless of where they stand. Even for longstanding clients, whenever you sense that a connection is strained, you can always apply extra energy and creativity to strengthen it. Running your agency in accordance with your innermost desires, and documenting and assessing the state of affairs regularly, on a personal basis, you can build something that is deeply rewarding, and immensely valuable.

Leadership and Management

A series of benchmarks can be used to identify well-managed clients with solid leadership. For starters, is it easy to learn about its mission, and does that factor into its operations in obvious ways? Bear in mind, the same way this focus offers a viable lens for your use in evaluating a prospect, it works both ways: Your own mission and your efforts to promote it are likely to attract suitors – or deflect them, depending upon mutual alignment.

To say the least, the exact nature of your engagements is subject to countless factors. A 2019 tweet I spotted offered some fascinating insights into people's vastly different perspectives when it comes to their work preferences.[1] It began with a statement attributed to self-described "venture hacker" Naval Ravikant, who is widely hailed as a luminary entrepreneur, investor, and tinkerer. This sentiment correlated happiness with working for small companies, praising the heightened creative liberties and interrelationships, and fewer restrictions.

Despite quickly earning over a thousand likes, the first commenter added a very real dimension, pointing out the obvious vulnerabilities if the group happens to be insane.

While the challenges that can hamper smaller companies were magnified in additional comments, I feel that those vulnerabilities also abound in larger corporate settings. Personally, I prefer to work with companies that have up to about 50 employees, where there is a better chance of interacting directly with the principals and being considered vital to operations. However, I fully understand that your ideas for applying this skill set and knowledge may lead you in other directions.

The illustrious Elise Mitchell and her self-named PR firm have been mentioned in these pages. With operations that span the globe, more than 100 employees and over U.S. $100 million in annual revenue, matching Ms. Mitchell's accomplishments is a real possibility for those who study her history and follow her lead. My friends who have dedicated themselves to establishing their expertise in the field of investor relations, for another example, may have started with a background and interests just like yours.

Knowing what you want, today, and understanding what is important to you, is a solid starting point.

To set your sights for the future, as part of your work, make it a habit to open yourself up to possibilities by reading books and magazines, and watching and listening to interviews and talks that interest you. When you spot someone who inspires you, follow that source of information to learn what you can about their ideas on leadership. Then, guide yourself forward by making a plan that uses your own ideas about what is most important in your business, and use that to present yourself professionally. Be authentic, but also bold and optimistic; confidence in positioning yourself in ways that befit your business heroes very well may lead you to connect with them.

Objectives

It may sound cliché, but people really do wind up riding in elevators together every day, and those semi-random, impromptu introductions really can present opportunities of a lifetime. If you can use such a short burst of time to learn about the objectives of a potential prospect, you will be in great position to present ideas that can put you in business together.

At the time when I was entering the full-time working world, I feel like it was a relatively new innovation for job candidates to include an objective on their resumes. Based on my experiences since then, I now encourage jobseekers to create a Leadership Brand statement for such applications; you can still call it an objective, it is just a bit more strategic. The point is, communicating your intent and your desires is a powerful means for fulfilling them, even though fruition can require much more time and effort than one would ever expect … and even then, there are no guarantees.

Here again, knowing how your own positioning can be essential in attracting partners with complementary needs, world views, values, etc., your own Leadership Brand should be used to evaluate opportunities. The next steps involve advancing your expertise in researching the objectives of others, and in strategizing means for fulfilling them. These keystone procedures from the POSTAR planning model, which also are pivotal in the often-referenced Copy Platform, apply to every engagement you will earn. If you can positively identify an objective for your client and substantiate that satisfying it is a priority for them, any effort on your part to address that aim is likely to be welcome.

Before graduating from college, I was interviewed for a job at one of Central Florida's largest post-production companies. The opening was for an account executive, and I was presented with this objective: We are looking for ways to attract local businesses for our services. Asked how I would go about addressing that and having no answers, the interview led nowhere. A couple of years later, I learned the same company was looking for a writer. My positioning and qualifications allowed me to easily formulate a strategy for fulfilling that need, and soon enough, the job was mine.

In 2019, I read about Mitchell Communications winning an account with a national non-profit organization focused on raising awareness for foster care, where Mitchell's stated role was to provide PR and earned media expertise in support of a major communications initiative.[2] That seems like another perfect example of an alignment of complementary business objectives … illustrating how the PR firm's own intent and desires match with those of the foundation.

Business Brands and Branding

When I think about personal branding, an experience from the early days of DWA often comes to mind. After sharing a proposal with a prospect, he offered constructive criticism on my font usage. In other early efforts aimed at establishing myself in the graphic design community, I encountered more feedback that was less than positive related to my website and some key messaging. While I do not consider myself to be an expert in branding, I have learned quite a bit over time. Among the imperatives:

1. Design elements should elegantly add or heighten core relevance and meaning.
2. Simplicity conveys finesse.
3. Consistency in usage and presentation is vital for brand integrity.
4. Certain design elements (like the font Comic Sans) can carry negative connotations that may require extensive education to be understood.

Thankfully, I was able to pick up tips and evolve my brand and design elements over time, to arrive at the place where my brand presence continues to be attractive in the design-heavy world where my business operates. Further, with the counsel of Everclear Marketing President and Founder G. Scott Shaw, I have learned how to present my business and myself more powerfully through storytelling, by virtue of regular updates to my owned and social media channels that are aligned with my mission, values, and brand. I also make better use of my customers' experiences in working with me, in the form of results, testimonials, and case studies presented in my materials.

Taking such lofty challenges to heart in the business world can certainly be daunting, which is why I have done my best to plunge you into them. While Everclear is Mr. Shaw's enterprise, you have encountered many variations in these pages. Another I have fond feelings for is Glossy, Inc., the Toronto-based imprint of Shannon Stephaniuk, which since 2006 has become well known for its accomplishments providing publicity and marketing specifically for advertising-related creative ventures. To the benefit of Glossy, on social media, Ms. Stephaniuk presents her professional feats in service of an amazingly impressive list of brands and artists.

Among all the superpowers unleashed by expert branding, StrawberryFrog Founder Scott Goodson lists differentiation at the top.[3] Distinction is the key to a company's financial success, he assures us, while also praising brands' abilities to drive behavior. From my perspective, it appears that Glossy has enjoyed solid prospects for long-term profitability, and I believe that success owes much to Ms. Stephaniuk's diligence and perseverance in building her brand and proactively putting it forward.

In summary, this aspect of business communications is so important that I feel a basic understanding of it is a requirement. You do not need expert certification but attaining such knowledge would surely be well rewarded. At the very least, you should comprehend this discipline well enough to be able to follow a client's branding guidelines to the letter, since your role is sure to involve brand guardianship and stewardship. Otherwise, when questioned on whether a given communications initiative is "on brand," you may fail a critical test of your worthiness to the title of chief communications officer.

Business Development

Among smaller enterprises, the job of sales usually falls to the principals – but over time, it is standard practice to enlist others in that role. When that salesperson comes along and is successful, it is often a game-changer for the company. It is no wonder individuals who master this alchemy are often referred to as *rainmakers*.

Regardless of the size of a business, those who bring the virtual rain – i.e., money – hold an inestimable amount of power and importance. After all, they manage the threshold where prospects stand to become coveted customers. However, if their efforts fail, institutional despair can quickly set in. In the case of feast or famine, supporting those responsible for business development is imperative.

Agency Management

Imagine a fruit stand that regularly sells out of inventory, and a competitor that sells none. It is easy to wonder what is wrong with the fruit at stand number two, or what is different about the vendor's sales approach. To get answers, questioning a few shoppers to see why they prefer the first, and to see if they have any opinion on the second, should help. Through that research, one might gain an insight that could improve the results of the struggling vendor; if that effort does not pay off, surely something else can be done, even if it means moving to a different location.

Although the sales functions of most businesses are bound to be more complicated than those faced by these small vendors, the basic processes of sales, and the actions that can be taken to support them, are common. If sales are high, a communications consultant adept in the key skill set can endeavor to learn what is working, and to use that information – along with the other core tenets of corporate communications, including the mission, the brand, the values, the customers – through storytelling and integrated marketing. By then continuing to monitor sales performance, those efforts can be adjusted to ensure they are impactful.

On the other hand, if sales are falling short, a communications consultant's research can take more of a SWOT (Strengths, Weaknesses, Opportunities, and Threats) approach, and the resulting promotional efforts are likely to be celebrated, especially if they prove effective.

Continuing to apply this fruit stand metaphor to other businesses – it also holds that if there are no sales, very quickly, there is no business. And, if the inventory sells out every day, there is considerable opportunity to grow, which may warrant additional planning and strategic action. In both cases, a proven communicator with a high I.Q. in marketing, driving intelligent, prescriptive promotions, can produce results that greatly exceed her fees.

Now, let's flip the script around to where the communications consultant is seeking to substantiate her value to the small business owner before being hired. As with the corporate rainmaker, if the consultant's objective is fulfilled, the result will be a new customer. To prepare, refresh yourself on all matters related to business development and the winning and managing of PR accounts. On day one of The Darnell Works Agency, I had the confidence of knowing that many companies need the proven communicator described immediately above. In fact, I felt certain that an infinite number of prospects existed, with most having a budget beyond U.S. $5,000 to pay for them, especially if the consultant is effective. As the rainmaker for DWA, my job was to get the check from those first willing customers.

All my experience aligned, and even though my first website did not pass muster with the venture capital investors of my first big client, I did get their money and their signature on my letter agreement … while closing numerous sales transactions in the first few weeks of my new venture. I feel it is worth noting the copy used on my business cards. I had a logo, and I used it along with The Darnell Works Agency, a NASA photo of an astronaut in space, and a tagline: Dynamic public relations. Under that, before providing my contact information, I used these words you will recognize.

Objectives

Strategies

Results

In the big picture of my small business, I feel the Chief Marketing Officer in me did great work for my Chief Executive Officer counterpart in this prescriptive promotional effort. For anyone who received this card and began to judge me and my services based on its verbiage, they would quickly think of their own objectives. They would see that I was positioning myself to offer strategies, and to generate results … with all three concepts building from the bottom-line objective. It is a paradigm that draws my prospects in very effectively and has worked wonders.

As you determine how best to draw in prospects for your agency, you are most welcome to use this verbiage. I will add my hope that you can successfully come through with the ROI and results your clients will require to win in business. If so, you will have mastered the ability to make rain.

Customer Service

This chapter's structure involves reiterating the importance of different aspects of business, and then turning the table to illuminate that aspect's equal value to your own enterprise. On the subject of customer service, what can be addressed and amplified that is not already crystal clear?

Quickly, let's dive into the "Patron of Customer Service" role you may need to fulfill in your client duties. Considering the fate of any company whose products or services fail, these scenarios very well might apply to your small, medium-sized, and bigger company clients, respectively.

1. Small: Of great use in marketing are the processes, people, and other innovations the company is using to create value for its clients.

2. <u>Medium:</u> Those who maintain the client relationships are often unsung heroes – you can be their champion if you can illuminate their importance in the company's success.
3. <u>Large:</u> Like your strong connection to sales, actively taking stock of the company's product and service offerings is a shrewd focus. What you learn is likely to bear on the results you can achieve, which might put you on the spot. If so, be prepared to make the case as to how much value there is for the company in what you are learning.

The notion of unsung heroes is one I feel is widely applicable to businesses, and it represents a primary target for you as you look for ways to add value for your clients. Despite the increasing awareness of customer engagement as a primary business objective, there are still plenty of under-valued customer service representatives toiling away in the shadows, taking great care of VIP customers. Seek inspiration in this insight and pursue its applicability to your clients' businesses … then find strategic ways to sing these heroes' praises.

At the same time, embrace the customer service patron role in your own business. After many months working at The Terpin Group, I noticed that the company's general manager seemed to be much more focused on landing new business compared with renewing our current clients. It was an obvious gaffe to me, evidenced each time I was asked to pitch a new client. If I was out on a pitch or preparing a proposal, how could I focus on my existing clients? It also followed that if today's effort could lead a roster client to extend their contract, I would not have time for a new client anyway. Current client work is billable, unlike time spent chasing a prospect.

Each of these insights absolutely inspired the way I have dedicated myself to my DWA clientele. After 22 years in business, having my average client engagement exceed 30 months is the customer service ROI I dreamt about when we left the mecca of Los Angeles for a small college town in North Carolina. Making my commitment known to my clients has become standard operating procedure. So, is it good design or good luck to have found so many worthy business partners? From my point of view, good fortune has arisen due to emphatically putting roster clients first.

Integrated Marketing

Bold brands assail us at every turn in the real world, presenting us with infinite examples of what integrated marketing looks like. Insurance companies seem to be among the biggest spenders on television; it is virtually impossible to escape their polished ad messages as we use our computers and phones, and as we navigate urban areas. You can probably recall a recent vehicle ad shown on TV, as well as the mobile, print, or outdoor rendition delivered to your field of view, as if by magic. Artificial intelligence is hammering away to bring smarter messages to your attention organically, with no end in sight for anyone living on the grid.

Over several decades, ATTIK created savvy advertising content for its far-ranging clientele. At one point while serving as the firm's press agent, I received an inquiry from a journalist asking why ad agencies do not advertise themselves. Presenting that to the agency's CEO led to a good if awkward laugh, and the query went unanswered. Had we chosen to explain ATTIK's integrated marketing approach, it would have sounded something like this.

In its culture and in action, ATTIK was always deeply committed to excellence, creativity, and brands. From its origination in 1986, it created leave-behind materials that crystallized these values in fascinating ways, which left readers spellbound. The principals were always ambitious in pitching themselves, and anything shown was always top tier. Given their truly brilliant portfolio of work and unchecked confidence, their version of integrated marketing leveraged branding, reputation management, sophisticated business development strategies, word-of-mouth and guerilla marketing, search engine optimization, and eventually, sponsorships, some paid registrations with the likes of AgencySpotter.com, and over a lifespan of nearly 30 years, a handful of ad placements. It is safe to say that even the most obscure and unproven marketing tactics were considered at one time or another, and when something felt right for the objectives, it was exploited masterfully, and cost-effectively.

ATTIK's story always featured its work, which included breathtaking original intellectual property that advanced institutional knowledge, skills, and proficiency according to internal values. In the creative industry, the firm's prolific "Noise" laboratory remains the stuff of legend. Though the company was ostensibly built to serve clients, the volume and quality of its monumental, self-driven output reveals much about its success.

Addressing Blair Enn's imperative of having his clients develop codified strategy models to substantiate and improve their unique value propositions – and reap the benefits for their businesses in terms of positioning and marketing – imagine having a book you publish, which is all about applying your unique point-of-view and talents in the creation of something original. If business goes well, you also will have case studies to use in telling your story of solving problems for your clients – and showing your work. With these two different types of ammunition, you have a powerful arsenal to use in attracting and winning business.

My advice is to be like ATTIK in these ways: Work hard to prove that you can produce something original that's interesting; demonstrate your desire to apply your skill set to others' benefit by engaging with those you can attract and endeavoring to collaborate, professionally; stick with it until the project bears fruit, then use all your energy to celebrate and feature that fruition in ways that tout your contributions strategically; treat your venture as something great, even in the early going; and, to gain attention, do what you must, making your beliefs evident, and presenting yourself and your offerings authentically and consistently.

Bear in mind also that the common denominator in marketing at any scale is SEO, which involves intelligent, strategic use of your owned and social media channels. Use those like an ace, to engage in ongoing education and demonstrate your knowledge to the world.

Cash Flow and Project Flow

It is always essential to take these two frameworks into account in planning your activities: For your clients and your own agency, any expenditure of a resource must be affordable, and the Return on Investment (ROI) must exceed the cost. That is the definition of sustainability, and I have yet to work for a company that is simply focused on expending resources without having something to show for it.

I am sure you also understand the corporate emphasis on managing activities on a project basis, especially where consultants are involved. Most astute management teams will endeavor to build their internal teams to account for every major business need, and this certainly applies to sales and marketing activities. In my experience, those interested in adding PR capabilities to their organizations seem to have a filter on their willingness to explore the possibilities, which translates into an openness toward engaging only on a project- or trial-basis. In other words, the value must be proven, and the company's commitment is contingent upon results or ROI.

Package these bottom lines together, and you have the prescription for the proper bearing in approaching your client relationships. You must convince your prospects that you can fulfill the need (objective) that sparks their interest in speaking with you. Your ability to operate cost-effectively on a project-basis to demonstrate your value and deliver ROI is how success in the partnership will be measured. To begin, they will need to know how they can end the agreement simply and easily, in the event things do not go well. Don't take it personally: Recalling the McNeill PR Triangle, this mindset reflects a company's self-doubt at least as much as any questions about your capabilities.

You have learned the tenets of deal-making and account management. Leveraging those while being wary of your client's bottom line, you can build success one project at a time. By persevering mindfully, your work can educate your clients on the benefits of sustaining and building upon your project activities, illustrating the proven principles of design thinking, and the never-ending needs of finding new mysteries and translating them into heuristics and algorithms. Put more simply, your contributions can easily reveal the secrets of your client's success and use them constructively.

When and if the day arrives where the client asks to wrap things up, it is bound to sting at least a bit. However, since this is a natural phenomenon common to malleable, multifaceted business relationships, addressing that final objective with great care is yet another solid investment into your future.

Investors and Investor Relations

As we have seen, formal investor relations for public companies – or for privately held "Alphas" which may have similar aspirations – require the highest level of communications diligence. For even the most nebulous start-up, whenever the desire to attract investors is raised, the approaches prescribed throughout this book are especially warranted.

For publicly traded companies like P&G, day-to-day performance impacts shareholder value. As such, it makes complete sense that investor relations professionals represent the Alphas of the communications profession. However, for those who can operate a profitable private enterprise where income regularly exceeds costs and plenty of banks are at-the-ready to provide capital on fair terms, why bother with investors at all?

In our hometown of Asheville, North Carolina, two companies provide interesting insights on this subject. In 2019, we watched as two very reputable, successful, and highly respected establishments changed owners. The first is Asheville Music Hall (AMH), a premier venue for live entertainment located in the city's bustling, historic downtown. The second is Avenue M, a popular restaurant on the north end of town that built a steady following in its neighborhood. For AMH, the reasons for selling had to do with stability and growth,[4] whereas at Avenue M, the hands-on owners were ready to capitalize on their investment and move on.

In both examples, I witnessed the diligent efforts applied in the years leading up to the ownership changes, which magnified the reputations of both operations and created buzz. Prior to selling, each entity had forged a business profile that was solid in every sense. Expanding out to other companies we have discussed, ATTIK was acquired in 2007, and Mitchell Communications was acquired in 2013. Those acquisitions of an ad agency and a PR firm, respectively, converted the previous owners into employees, for a few years, until their contracts ended. At those points, the principals were able to pursue other ventures.

Whether a privately held company's goals have to do with stability, growth, or the opportunity to move on, engaging strategic communications capabilities and putting them to work is big league. Of course, for any business wishing to be considered above average, maintaining similarly high operational standards is shrewd. Following this counsel through, you are encouraged to view your consultancy as an above-average business, and to operate it such a way that it is worthy of investors, should you decide to grow or even sell it someday. This rationale provides even more validation for learning everything you can about investor relations: That knowledge is virtually guaranteed to impact your clients' businesses, and your own.

Reporting

When a person wants to meaningfully conclude a discussion, one will commonly hear these words: "At the end of the day ..." While the expression is often overused, it does convey some gravitas. Like days, most projects have a clear beginning and end, and once again, committing to engaging on a project-basis is agreeable to many entrepreneurs and managers, given the propensity of it coming to an end.

In my way of doing business, where I engage clients on an ongoing basis under the auspices of a letter agreement which proceeds month-to-month, there is a regular culmination which concludes each period, represented by a message, a report, and an invoice.

Do you agree that "the arena" illuminated in this chapter is important for you to understand and leverage in operating your consultancy? How essential are the aspects of leadership, management, objectives, branding, business development, customer service, integrated marketing, cash flow, project flow, and investor relations as they apply to companies you anticipate working with? Think for a minute about distilling down everything you will have done for a client into the report you will provide as you simultaneously ask to continue and request further payment. If you sense that the future of the relationship is at stake in the moments immediately after you send that report, we think alike.

When I worked at The Terpin Group, Lori-Ann Harbridge had the vital mission of helping account executives prepare our period-ending reports for our clients. This fact was brought home as each period wound down, putting her on-the-spot to gather and analyze results. She was extremely conscientious about these efforts, and at times when we were caught up in other activities – to the great benefit of the firm's bottom line, she was an unstoppable force. Regardless of how you choose to characterize the process of reporting to your clients, I hope you can conjure a similarly focused and strategic willpower. It is nothing less than your opportunity to keep your business afloat by convincing your clients to stick with you.

Even in the best situations after transmitting your report, you might receive a reply as simple as, "Thanks." So long as the response does not translate into "Stop," you are entitled to savor the fact that your clients are as committed as they can be to pursuing their objectives with you, moving into the future. That is how a successful communications consultant's client relationships work, at the end of the day.

Exploration

1. Why treat a sole-practitioner consultancy as an important business? List three good reasons and write a paragraph to explain each one.
2. How does having one client help attract another client, even if the first is pro-bono?
3. How do you position your consultancy when your firm does not appear anywhere in O'Dwyer's list of top agencies?
4. Make a list with the following sub-headings and write a short description of their importance for your business: reputation management; ethics; creativity; strategy; personal brand; business branding; the consulting mindset.
5. Write a multi-page journal entry where you discuss the present status and prospects for your business. Archive that so it you can easily find it in the future. Consider doing this weekly, or even more often, especially when things feel chaotic.

6. Describe the top three actual or anticipated benefits to your business to come from journaling.
7. Find someone you have no intention of working with for the foreseeable future, talk with them about how strategic communications might benefit their business and invite them to keep in touch.
8. What do you feel is the best size for a client company for you? Explain your choice and defend the suggestion that a company of a different size might offer better opportunities.
9. Knowing what you know, how can you leverage your Leadership Brand to attract great clients?
10. Using the "objectives, strategies, results" paradigm, formulate at least three examples you can use to present your offerings. If you cannot yet substantiate results, engage in pro-bono efforts until you can demonstrate your ability to successfully meet business objectives.

Notes

1 Route2FI. (2019, July 6). Route2FI on Twitter. Twitter. https://twitter.com/Route2FI/
2 Barnes, S. (2019, July 3). Mitchell Works with FosterMore. ODwyerpr.com. http://bit.ly/mitchFM
3 Goodson, S. (2012, May 30). Why Brand Building Is Important. Forbes. http://bit.ly/buildBR
4 Lunsford, M. (2019, May 23). Sold: Asheville Music Hall and The One Stop to brewery owner, local business broker. The Citizen-Times. http://bit.ly/AMH_19

7
Professional Development

Contemplating everything it takes to effectively operate as a freelance communications officer for numerous entrepreneurs and organizations, the importance of strategic thinking commands attention. Generating targeted media exposure begins with strategic planning, while the related activities of researching, relationship building, pitching, promoting – and managing client relations with an emphasis on high quality service – all require mindful discretion and diligence. Add in the efforts to ensure clients understand how PR complements and heightens all other aspects of marketing, and then maximizing our results, and you have a relatively complete picture of this valuable and profitable career track, where calculated plotting lights the way.

To navigate this path successfully, determine what you want to do and who you want to be, and move forward in those directions as methodically as possible. This is also true: Remaining effective requires constant improvement.

In the big picture, I encourage you to cultivate and successfully maintain inner peace, work-life balance, good health, to stay relatively well informed on day-to-day events of the world, and to know where you stand on topical issues occurring on your home and business fronts. When it comes to this job, each day should involve spending some time learning how to be a better resource for one's clients. Toward that goal, it is easy to recommend certain practices.

1. Read the publications you are regularly pitching for your clients, or those your clients wish to appear in (Tip: Subscribe to their email newsletters, usually free; due to your professional role in PR, many trade publications will also provide you with complimentary subscriptions).
2. Research competitors of your business and your clients; study what they are doing and consider engaging in activities that are similar – or

perhaps, completely different (Tip: Use Twitter Lists to confidentially gather up-to-date intelligence data on competitors).
3. Study the trades of the PR profession to see what subjects industry leaders are writing about and examine their prescriptions for success (Tip: Again, email subscriptions as well as highly instructive webinars are often no-cost).
4. Take time to regularly spill out your thoughts in the form of a journal. Doing so will reveal your concerns, which you will be wise to actively address.

If our world never changed, we could probably get by without learning anything new, as dull as that sounds. As a consultant aiming to positively impact others' businesses, maintaining up-to-date insight into the bedrock tenets of business success, as well as every facet of the communications consultant's key skill set, is a prerequisite. To be clear, I am not just talking about knowledge or opinions, although both are important; you need to be able to reference valid experiences that relate to today's concerns for your clients. Whether a colleague calls me her press agent, PR partner, representative or publicist, she relies on me for specialized communications expertise combined with the ability to create strategically sound content we introduce to the world. Yesterday, maybe we demonstrated that expertise, and something came out representing the client's Holy Grail. Now it is today: What's next?

Our work occurs in the proximity of the hallowed news business, where notoriously hard-working journalists toil away to make names for themselves and earn their keeps. Here, knowledge of yesterday is essential, but the emphasis is usually on reporting today's updates and tomorrow's possibilities. Trade media form isolated bands outside the mainstream, where the particulars of pop culture, politics or regional events may factor less, officially. Still, if you are seeking to establish familiarity and credibility with any working member of the press, leveraging common geophysical and cultural experiences only makes sense.

Finding the Diligence-Driven Demand

At the beginning of 2009, I was especially focused on business matters for The Darnell Works Agency. In the previous month, I had lost my bid to win a prestigious account based in Berkeley, California, and because of writing a detailed journal entry almost every day, I was mindful of needing to improve my marketing presence. By that time, I had been publishing a blog for over three years, where I was exercising my writing strengths and amplifying my point-of-view relatively successfully. Until then, I had called the blog MarSciTechTainment, an obvious if clunky amalgamation. Inspired by the inauguration of Barack Obama as President of the United States of America, I renamed the blog Universal Positive. As a channel for distilling my perspective and brand and allowing me to publish stories supporting existing clients while also engaging prospects, it instantly grew in effectiveness under the new banner.

Also at this time, the phenomenon known as Twitter was coming on strong in my niche of industry. Many of my clients were eager to have their work covered in the AdRants.com trade blog, and articles written by Publisher Steve Hall and his colleagues were increasingly obsessed with Twitter and its usage. With each new day, the newsletter's stories might focus on the platform's growing user-base, experimentation with ad placements, or other interesting developments any of us could experience ourselves by getting onboard. After ignoring what seemed to be a frivolous waste of time for as long as possible, I finally decided I had no choice but to wade in and begin educating myself.

Looking back, I am generally proud of how I handled these experiments, where I hoped to improve my knowledge and gain valuable experience without wasting time. As one measure of success, my annual sales for 2009 went up by ten percent compared with the previous year … then increased by thirteen percent the next year. Today, I consistently use Facebook, LinkedIn, Instagram, Pinterest, Tumblr, and Medium – as well as Twitter – to strategically promote my business. However, Twitter is arguably the most important social network for my business. Here are five amazing benefits of using Twitter.

1. Intelligence: Most journalists and media outlets have Twitter accounts. I can always see what's trending across the platform (and therefore, topical in popular culture), and what anyone using the platform is focusing on.
2. With Lists, I can compile public or private collections of accounts. When viewed on the platform, a list will reveal up-to-date output from any listed account, which is highly valuable for competitive assessment, niche research, and much more.
3. With Moments, I can create and curate a string of tweets and turn that into a stand-alone piece of content that can be embedded on other platforms and used as part of a pitch or feature story.

4. Paid promotions allow targeted content to be distributed to audiences that can be highly segmented – where the results can be analyzed extensively to assess effectiveness.
5. With diligence, a substantial following can be accrued over time, and the hands-on knowledge of what works and what doesn't is extremely valuable as a skill set that can be applied for others. Also, your Twitter account can be used to promote others and build relationships.

Without question, the expertise I have developed in using social media factors into my business affairs every day. Diving in was not easy for me, nor did it feel natural at first; and yet, I was rewarded very quickly for virtually every second invested.

If you commit yourself deeply to providing excellent communications support for your clients, and you leap into the work each day to advance their objectives strategically and creatively, you are going to encounter barriers to success that will be impossible to ignore. Maybe it will be a new social media platform that is being discussed, a conference shaping-up where attendance may be warranted, a new website in the works that your client wants to promote, a white paper being written that company executives feel will open doors to new customers, or the desire to place a story in the New York Times.

Your willingness to learn new tricks and lead communications accordingly is a standing qualification for success. While the uncertainty involved may be intimidating, the knowledge gained blazing new trails will raise your confidence – and your value among your clients.

Researching the Media

After many years of engaging with the media on the daily, my number one recommendation for successfully interfacing with any media outlet or reporter is to gain familiarity. People are generally inundated with information nowadays, and given the importance of their jobs as reporters, journalists are understandably finicky when it comes to the ways in which they can be approached, especially if someone is trying to pitch them a story. Having a solid understanding of their interests and the nuances of the outlet they work for is imperative.

Early in my career when I was submitting creative writing to literary magazines, I would spend hours reviewing entries in the newest annual "Writer's Market" edition I could get my hands on. Some listings were long and detailed, others quite sparse. Regardless, success with any seemed to demand following whatever guidelines they provided, to the letter. Among the litany of pet peeves spelled out, most shamed writers who failed to familiarize themselves with the publication, its style, and its audience. Fast forward to year 2000 at The Terpin Group (TTG), where I further confirmed that a sure way to get a journalist to respond (negatively) was to pitch something off-topic.

One might make the case that digitalization has made it easier than ever to research media outlets directly. Between publications' own websites and a handful of social media platforms, learning about almost any media outlet, comprehending its style, and analyzing its coverage is short work. My time at TTG coincided with the full-blown ascendency of the Internet. Until then, we were still using the massive, printed catalogs sold by Bacon's Information, providing listings similar to the Writer's Market annuals. Bacon's had already adopted disc-based publication as well, and web-based directories were soon to come. In other words, when a PR pro wanted to get up-to-speed on a media outlet, they would go to a printed Bacon's guide, or to an offline database, where all the information (accurate or not) was premium in nature … meaning access was expensive. Since then, that data has moved online, where it can often be accessed freely through due diligence and savvy thinking.

What I have just described covers a period of history where fortunes were made and lost, and where PR professionals and journalists alike invested massive amounts of time, energy, and money, resulting in methodologies and workflows which have shapeshifted. In 2003, the highly accomplished PR professional B.L. Ochman published an article on her blog, chronicling a large-scale business move from Bacon's, which had just acquired a competitor.[1] Her story provided a fascinating time-capsule, revealing her leadership in surveying the viable options then available to other pros seeking accurate information on media contacts, and offering to share her hard-earned insights in exchange for a small fee.

According to Hoovers.com (a product of Dun & Bradstreet), Bacon's Information began as a news clipping service in 1932, and it was acquired by the Sweden-based research firm Cision AB in 2001, before being re-branded in 2007 as Cision US.[2] Notably, Cision also acquired PR Newswire for over U.S. $800 million in 2016, demonstrating the value of providing software and services for PR and marketing professionals. Unsurprisingly, today, any PR pro wanting to get up-to-speed on a media outlet can still purchase information through Cision, through its top competitor BusinessWire (a subsidiary of

Warren Buffett's Berkshire Hathaway, Inc.), or through any number of other firms seeking their share of this rich marketplace.

Bear in mind, the info being pedaled is subject to being out-of-date as soon as a reporter switches beats or jobs. Although Cision and its competitors have ready answers for that problem, this is just another reason why I personally focus on doing my own media research, and why my take is included here. Regardless of my opinion, this is yet another inescapable reality of this profession: There are tools designed to make you more efficient in your job, and it is up to you to explore them and determine for yourself whether they are worthwhile.

Taking this to heart, in 2020, I inquired about access to Cision's database. Of course, they wanted to sell me on the Cision Communications Cloud described in the following links. As you can see, this magnificent product exists to address all the key aspects of this job laid out in the chapter opening.

- Introducing Cision Communications Cloud: https://youtu.be/L5SOqzT0rA4
- Planit's Cision Communications Cloud Case Study: https://cisn.co/2si5Q4G
- Cision Communications Cloud Analysis: https://www.capterra.com/p/129611/Cision/

When I explained that I was just interested in access to the database, the rate quoted for that was about U.S. $300 per month. Although I have not inquired, I would guess that full access is closer to U.S. $800 per month, billed annually (reportedly, it varies according to company size). Over time, I have also evaluated research and pitching services from Muck Rack, and monitoring and analysis services from Meltwater and TrendKite. All offer powerful tools for measuring the success of communications efforts and are well worth exploring, when you feel the investments varying from hundreds to thousands of dollars per month can be impactful in your client engagements. If you have an Alpha client that favors a Flush or a Steady Strategy, you should strongly consider all tools like these.

Otherwise, with your clients' needs in mind, make time to educate yourself on what is happening in the media today. Subscribing is one option, but you can also go to the library or to a bookstore where you can browse. Subscribe to free newsletters offered by relevant media outlets and scan them as a regular part of your day. Extend your skills and your relationships through social media, and actively improve your abilities to pitch and promote, creatively and strategically. On the subject of the media, using your owned and social media channels, assert your knowledge in your communications and advance your own reputation as a scholar – and, where appropriate, as an expert.

Trade Associations

In college, I took up the reigns of my university's cinematography association. The extracurricular experiences I gained forming up and leading more than 100 students took my education and my industry contacts to higher levels. One of the guest speakers I lined up was producer, director, and director of photography Randy Baker. Several years later, Mr. Baker was one of the first to hire me in a freelance capacity. At the end of a day shooting video on location, Mr. Baker informed me of his need to make a stop on the way back into town and invited me to join him. We soon arrived at Nickelodeon Studios on the Universal Studios Florida backlot, where my host was appointed as the new President of the Orlando Chapter of the International Television Association (ITVA).

Thanks to that introduction, I wound up serving as Public Relations Chairman for ITVA Orlando from 1993 to 1995, where we proudly brought home Chapter of the Year honors in 1995. There again, the time and effort were extracurricular to my job, but it also provided a high-profile platform for me, which was invaluable in building my reputation, my network, and ultimately, expertise in my field.

The many organizations that draw legions of communications professionals together include The Chartered Institute of Public Relations, The International Public Relations Association, The Public Relations Consultants Association, and The Public Relations Society of America.

While the ITVA no longer exists, DWA client companies maintain affiliations with the American Institute of Graphic Arts (AIGA), the American Marketing Association (AMA), the Association of Independent Commercial Producers (AICP), Promax, the Association of Computing Machinery's Special Interest Group on Computer Graphics and Interactive Techniques (SIGGRAPH), The Audiovisual and Integrated Experience Association (AVIXA), The National Association of Broadcasters (NAB), The Society for Experiential Graphic Design (SEGD), The Society of Digital Agencies (SoDA), and The Themed Entertainment Association (TEA), among others. Most municipalities offer some type of Chamber of Commerce, and Meetup.com is yet another way to investigate opportunities to apply oneself,

Professional Development 115

learn new things, and build meaningful connections that can lead to career ignition and rejuvenation. It is yet another field where being creative and strategic can yield phenomenal results for you, and that is bound to translate into higher value for your clients.

Industry Gatherings

Running through the list of industry associations above provides a highly effective means for me to share the career ROI I have generated through participation in gatherings, whether on my clients' behalf, or my own.

- 1989–1990 – UCF Cinematography Association: As President, handled all aspects of recruiting board members, organizing, promoting (including publishing newsletter and flyers) and running board meetings, inviting and liaising with VIP guests, and hosting monthly gatherings and other special events.
- 1993–1995 – International Television Association, Orlando Chapter: As Public Relations Chairman, participated in board meetings, and promoted (including publishing and handling distribution for flyers) monthly gatherings and other special events.
- 1998–1999 – AFI, Hermosa Beach, Malibu, Santa Barbara, and Slamdance International Film Festivals: Representing Crest National Labs, established and managed sponsorships, including exhibiting, and presenting awards to winners.
- 1999–2003 – PromaxBDA Annual Conferences: Attended conferences in San Francisco, San Jose, New Orleans, New York, and Los Angeles in support of DWA and clients.
- 2001 – The CLIO Awards: Attended industry gathering in Miami Beach in support of DWA client Endless Noise.
- 2001-present – AICP Show, Tour, East/West Coast Holiday Events and Selected Regional Events: Attended these commercial production industry gatherings in support of DWA and clients, several of whom were sponsors.

I will stop there – but I am sure you understand my point. In the years since, if I have had a client speaking at or attending a conference I can attend, I consider joining them. And whenever a client hosts an original event and invites me to join the fun, I accept the invitation if the conditions are favorable. Generally, so long as I can bill a couple of hours for the meeting time, I will cover my own travel and accommodation costs. Locally and regionally, certain causes and groups have earned my pro-bono support of their communications and events, from time to time. Across the board, I have always found that the connections made face-to-face, and the relationships built and fortified in-person are generally on a higher level than what can be achieved by phone, email, and teleconference.

With all of this in mind, I encourage you to look for suitable opportunities to get out, shake hands, "press the flesh," and invest in real-world relationship-building, whenever doing so stands to produce considerable benefits for you or your clients. If it is possible to take a leadership position, the results can be especially beneficial.

Further Resources

Given the nature of change, specific programs, and offerings I suggest here are subject to disappearing by the time you are encountering this information. Still, these are the types of pursuits that can inspire you, transform your skills and open new doors, professionally and socially.

1. Academic Programs
2. Professional Education
3. Extracurricular Activities

Whether you participate in-person or online, the professionals employed by universities and colleges all around the world stand ready to boost your education in countless ways, where degrees and other certifications are among the sure rewards of your scholarship. Promotions for new program offerings from certain institutions always pique my interest. Even if your financial means seem to preclude involvement with the likes of Stanford, UC Berkeley, Harvard, Columbia, or some other school, I encourage you to sign up for their mailing lists or other periodicals they offer, and to follow their social media accounts. Perhaps the forces will align, and the perfect program of study will appear within your sights at an opportune time; otherwise, even summaries from their published research can heighten your superpowers by identifying worthy subjects and courses of study you can pursue on your own.

Many of the same schools that operate degree programs now offer studies in the category of professional education. Then there are non-accredited academic institutions, many of which are highly respected in their fields. In the creative industry, I have been intrigued by certification programs I have seen offered by various schools in fields like Animation, Graphic Design,

Branding, Brand Strategy, SEO for Designers, Marketing and Creative Business Entrepreneurship. To research this further to suit your interests, search for "best non-accredited certification programs."

The chapter on Investor Relations presented details on training provided by the National Investor Relations Institute. The institute's website (https://www.niri.org) is an opulent resource for communications professionals to explore further opportunities for career development. Here are six others I expect to stand ready to help us meet our professional education needs, well into the future.

- https://www.prsa.org
- http://www.ragantraining.com
- https://www.prweek.com
- https://www.ipra.org
- https://www.cipr.co.uk
- https://www.prca.org.uk

Exploration

Right now, and every workday hereafter, spend 10 minutes apiece on items 1–7 below.

1. Improve your ability to generate targeted media exposure for your clients.
2. Improve your ability to build relationships with media professionals and influencers.
3. Improve your ability to pitch stories to the media.
4. Improve your ability to promote your clients.
5. Improve the service you provide to your clients.
6. Improve your clients' understanding of the ways PR complements and heightens all other aspects of their marketing.
7. Maximize the results and ROI of your campaign efforts for your clients.
8. Each year, ad industry maven and luminary Cindy Gallop uses her Twitter account to live-tweet as she reads through the September issue of Vogue Magazine.[3] List and explain three reasons why this is probably a brilliant expenditure of her valuable time.
9. Pick a print issue of any magazine that appeals to you and spend an hour reviewing its contents. Afterward, list five things you learned and think about how that knowledge can benefit you, moving forward.
10. Participate in one free or paid webinar per month for the next three months and consider attending an industry gathering before the end of

this year. If you have a Twitter account, use it strategically to raise the value of these efforts. If you do not have a Twitter account, either set one up now and begin using it, or explain your choice to skip it for now.

Notes

1 Ochman, B. L. (2003, December 6). Bacon's Acquires Media Map: Start of a Shake Up? What's Next? Blog. http://bit.ly/WNBacon
2 Dun & Bradstreet. (n.d.). Cision US Inc. Company Profile. Dnb.com. Retrieved May 24, 2021, from http://bit.ly/CisionUS1
3 Gallop, C. (2020, September 7). Cindy Gallop on Twitter. http://bit.ly/CGV_20

8
Scaling and Exit Strategies and Tactics

Fortunately for me, the career inspiration kick-started by the U.S. Air Force's "Aim High" campaign has led to solid, sustainable success. With Beth Darnell's vital support, and a handful of consultants and other service companies at our beck and call, the track record for the business and its clients represents a formidable win-win. Hopefully, you are also seeing this as a business model you can own, personalize, and build upon.

Over time, I have come to know many sole-practitioners in this field, as well as others who have decided to grow their businesses – leading to even greater rewards. Although DWA has operated with the minimal number of human resources, I believe I am in a unique position to guide you in exploring the rationales and strategies for expansion, and some of the most viable tactics.

Another U.S. military marketing slogan heightens motivations for this subject. To me, as the principal of a business built upon the efforts of a single practitioner, it is virtually impossible to imagine anyone buying it from me. When we start to seriously think about having an entity that some other might take interest in purchasing, building out the enterprise with more staff members seems to be a necessity. Therefore, to capitalize on your investments into your consultancy – and in the spirit of the U.S. Army, "Be All You Can Be" – you may have no choice but to scale.

Why Scale?

When I first met Karen Raz, the principal of Raz Public Relations in Los Angeles, it was because she had hired one of my former colleagues from The Terpin Group (TTG) to be part of her staff. Since then, I have watched as she has demonstrated the benefits of having multiple, extremely qualified PR professionals representing her firm, building their business together

DOI: 10.4324/9781003177913-12

and making vital contributions to the success of their clients. While there is some overlap in our client lists, Ms. Raz's expanded bandwidth and capabilities make her a better fit for many businesses, especially those with interests that can be well served by individuals in LA who can physically attend meetings and events.

In 2006, another competitor's developments grabbed my attention, when a few sole practitioners joined forces to launch a PR firm in New York and LA. Given their size, their expertise, and their physical presence in major markets, I have referred companies to them at times, I have lost more than one account to them, and once, they offered me a job. The examples of competitive companies in my field growing and achieving success of higher magnitudes go on and on.

During my TTG era, where I was one of six account professionals working with the general and office managers in LA who also billed their time, we came close to billing U.S. $1 million annually. That is nearly seven times more than what I have billed in a year, on average, since leaving TTG in 2000. What is important to remember in analyzing those numbers is that my salary at TTG was about U.S. $1,000 per week. Applying the same pay rate for the other seven staffers, that adds up to U.S. $416,000 per year, or far less than half of the annual billings. In other words, by scaling TTG, Mr. Terpin had a considerable opportunity for income that he did not have to earn himself. Worth mentioning, TTG also had offices in New York and San Francisco.

For further comparison, note that between 2001 and 2010, DWA's annual billings doubled. While this reflects a rate increase of U.S. $25 per hour over that span, the growth was primarily based on higher confidence and improved efficiency in handling multiple accounts. This represents yours truly maximizing earning potential within the sole-practitioner model. Throughout the life of my business, non-clients have readily suggested that I staff up. Assessing that possibility, I have estimated that I could probably bill qualified colleagues at a rate twice as high as their hourly costs, and if all went well, find myself in Mr. Terpin's position described above. Still, I am so mindful of the anticipated impact on my day-to-day affairs that scaling has remained unattractive. Most often, I have expressed this as me loving what I do, which does not involve managing other people. At TTG, GM Mike Garfinkel earned my respect hiring, managing, and babysitting account executives like me, and replacing them when necessary. He also had to regularly pursue new accounts to keep everyone occupied. Meanwhile, here at DWA, it also matters greatly to me that when I am doing my work for my clients, I am earning my rate ... whereas in managing other account professionals, at least in the early going, I would not be.

Even with so much validation for my solo business preferences, reading about Elise Mitchell selling her company to Dentsu got my undivided attention. Knowing of our common roots in PR, I could not help but feel challenged by the achievements of Ms. Mitchell and her business partners. Her book "Leading Through the Turn" offers a lot of intelligence into her unique talents, experiences and drives, and the specific ways she applied them to build her firm into a powerhouse.

If you have any doubts about the uniqueness of every human being, look at the 34 individual traits listed in the world famous CliftonStrengths assessment.[1] This analytical system categorizes the different themes into four domains: Influencing, Executing, Strategic Thinking, and Relationship Building. Knowing the high probability of measuring higher or lower in those domains, it makes sense that each of us has passion for things like managing others, pursuing new business, planning strategically, or completing assignments.

At the time of this writing, our cousin Michelle Schwab is achieving considerable success with her firm Orchard Point Group, which is based in Cary, North Carolina. She has a staff of several very accomplished account professionals, and according to her, using the CliftonStrengths assessment and applying its insights has been mission critical. For example, Ms. Schwab understands that her own key strength is in Executing ... and when she is going to meet a new client, she is sure to take along her Relationship-Building ace, who scored especially high in the trait of "Woo."

The CliftonStrengths assessment is included in the book, "Now, Discover Your Strengths" from psychologist and author Donald O. Clifton, Ph.D., and coauthor Marcus Buckingham. Mr. Buckingham is responsible for a related toolset, the StandOut Assessment, and between the two gentlemen, many books and resources exist to help us all better understand ourselves and others and aim accordingly.

The DiSC Profile is a simple exercise anyone can complete to gain insights into their unique behavioral tendencies.[2] Since it evaluates one's acuity around the pillars of Dominance, Influence, Steadiness and Conscientiousness, knowing your DiSC style can reveal knowledge that is wise to address. Obviously, this knowledge can also be essential for maximizing group and solo pursuits.

Among the participants in the 2012 Recourses New Business Summit I attended was Josh Kohnstamm, then owner of the highly rated Minnesota-based PR firm Kohnstamm Communications, with whom I share a common love for the merits of our profession. A quote I once spotted on his website exulted in PR's abilities to fully unleash brand powers consistently, which drives expansion, draws in business partners and star recruits, and helps to crush competition.

In late 2019, Kohnstamm Communications was acquired by a company named Broadhead. Reportedly, the deal came about due to Mr. Kohnstamm's personal desire to focus on business growth while simultaneously availing his clients of Broadhead's expanded creative and studio services.[3] This seems to be a classic case of two specialized firms with complementary expertise joining forces to the potential benefit of each other's clients.

Despite so many examples of companies in my marketplace that have successfully grown, understanding everything it takes to be successful even as a sole-practitioner, I have held fast. After all, not only do I have to be committed to ongoing learning to be a great resource to my clients every day, I also must champion my personal and business brands, and treat DWA as a client, experimenting and evolving in my profession. Even with expert support, financial and other enterprise-related affairs – for example, Information Technology demands – require regular vigilance. With my family values and desire for optimal work-life balance, being bigger holds no interest, and selling my business has seemed neither achievable nor necessary.

Through 2019, this all held true; and yet, as discussed previously, things change. In a 2014 TED Talk, scholar, professor, and author Daniel Gilbert dismantles the human propensity to believe we generally remain the same over time.[4] Building on that insight, Jen Kim's 2019 article for Psychology Today[5] connects it with self-actualization, the highest basic need for our species, according to Abraham Maslow. This compulsion points us ever onward in the same direction as the *be all we can be* mantra – assuming we have first satisfied our physiological, safety, belongingness, and self-esteem requirements, in that order.[6]

For each of us, making the right decision for today is the imperative, but being open to change very well might result in some magic for our future selves. Having carried this belief for many years, exposure to the wisdom of interior designer Ilse Crawford in the original Netflix series "Abstract: The Art of Design" opened an unexpected door. As I understand it, the emphasis of her work is on improving human experiences. When she and her colleagues are successful in their design approaches, the result is often a solution that can scale, thereby creating opportunities to improve experiences for more people.

While making my business bigger for its own sake, making more money, and selling my business all seem tedious, risky, and at least somewhat selfish and wonky to me, the idea of improving the offerings to generate <u>more positive experiences for more prospects</u> has weight. The transactions I have mentioned in the acquisitions of Kohnstamm Communications and Mitchell appear to meet that criterion. In the next facets of this discussion, we will explore business growth in more detail ... and see how succession planning can illuminate some elevated opportunities.

Scaling Strategies and Tactics

There are more insights to be gleaned from the examples I have previously shared on competitors and clients who have grown their businesses exponentially. In "Leading Through the Turn," Ms. Mitchell describes a series of momentous events in her career. After leaving a multi-person consultancy – where she had done everything right, including earning a master's degree at night, and dedicated herself to her local chapter of the Public Relations Society of America (PRSA) by serving as its president – she and her husband set their sights on a new market. It was no easy decision, but Ms. Mitchell seized that setting to launch her own agency. I cannot possibly summarize all the expert, intelligent career and leadership counsel contained in her book, which she took to heart, applied, and shared, so I encourage you to read it for yourself. However, several fundamental steps seem especially powerful, and repeatable.

1. She invested herself into her new community by joining the local Chamber of Commerce, Junior League and Junior Service League, attending and leading their functions while diligently pursuing the best of those new relationships – and by reengaging with PRSA in the region, ultimately going on to launch and lead a new chapter.
2. Having retained one key client for her start-up consultancy prior to relocating, she then pursued and eventually landed more top-tier clients in her new region.
3. Slowly but surely, she built a network of accomplished professionals who were willing and able to work remotely, then applied her highly advanced leadership skills magnificently, to create a supportive, cohesive

culture. Ms. Mitchell listed 12 senior-level professionals in her agency's remote network by its tenth year in business.
4. With her first full-time hire, she recruited a highly accomplished competitor with his own lofty ambitions and deep determination to build a phenomenal company.
5. Here is what I refer to as Darnell's Law: Every new development, good or bad, is half challenge and half opportunity. Ms. Mitchell demonstrates its applicability at a rocky point in late 2008, due to the U.S. economic recession. Her optimism and leadership made a difference, in tandem with some extremely hard work. She reveals three key maneuvers (acknowledge your blindspots, build a stronger team and system, and use those strengths to full advantage[7]) as the reasons she was able to capitalize on the downturn, and more than triple annual revenues over the next two years.

If you have in mind to build a company that is going to maximize your time and efforts, and bring about maximum positive impact for your clients, I cannot think of a better person to study than Elise Mitchell. Her book is an absolute master class in what our business careers can look like if we are savvy, intelligent, determined, brave, and maybe a little lucky here and there (bearing in mind, good fortune favors the brave).

To me, bravery was a key ingredient in ATTIK's growth over its 29-year trajectory. From humble origins in Northern England in 1986, also leveraging connections made at the local chamber of commerce, the enterprising Co-Founders Simon Needham and James Sommerville had built solid word of mouth, and a team of eight, by 1990. According to the company's retrospective appearing in "Noise Five," written by the noted branding and marketing industry journalist Karl Greenberg, ATTIK was virtually bankrupt in 1991.[8] The wild fluctuations continued through its 2007 acquisition by Dentsu, and right up until 2015, when the venture wholly dissolved into its parent company's balance sheet. Here are more of the firm's big milestones.

- By early 1995, through fierce dedication to customer service, business development and its own brand culture, ATTIK's Huddersfield operation grew to 25 employees.
- That same year, the company self-published the first edition of Noise, its ambitious leave-behind print piece representing its unbridled ambitions and capabilities. It became ATTIK's entrée into London and the city's high-caliber clientele.
- ATTIK soon launched its London office, and the second edition of Noise.

- ATTIK's mid-1996 foray into New York City was exploratory and bold. Armed with 24 copies of Noise 3, the introductory trip was haphazard but productive. After six months servicing the NYC clients they had met (and shapeshifting to begin creating designs in motion), partner Will Travis opened the New York office.
- Offices four and five commenced in San Francisco and Sydney in 1999, requiring even more focused business development diligence, and more expansion of core capabilities.
- At the end of 2000, ATTIK was reportedly billing U.S. $21 million annually, with more than 200 staff members and five offices. The company was also deeply in-debt and addicted to a project-based business model where its relationships with agencies (versus being brand-direct) left it highly vulnerable.
- On September 11, 2001, Mr. Sommerville and Mr. Travis watched in horror from a NYC rooftop as the tragic events seen around the world unfolded. The omnipotent destruction brought business to a standstill, and several months later, ATTIK advisor Ric Peralta enlightened all global stakeholders to the harsh realities and began restructuring.
- By the end of 2002, ATTIK closed all offices but Huddersfield and San Francisco, and cut its staff back to 45.
- The next few years were difficult. By focusing on profitability, core strengths, customer service and business development – fully leveraging the group's youth marketing expertise and its innovative approaches to integrated marketing in its positioning – it began landing the right kind of business, including Toyota's Scion account in 2003.

ATTIK's rollercoaster ride continued, and I was an integral part of it from 2002 to 2014. At different stops along the way, as they stretched to do more or recoiled to recharge, the strategies and tactics were all over the map. To me, a fascinating dimension stems from the fact that, throughout its journey, ATTIK's story also reflects the groundbreaking work delivered for its clients. Clearly, those deliverables represent major marketing initiatives for brands (and their business partners, including many ad agencies) at key moments in their histories. There are profound lessons to be learned from the results of ATTIK's track record, and those of its clients.

For example, Toyota's strategy with Scion was to bring younger buyers into its product family. The dazzling array of campaigns deployed by Scion in tandem with ATTIK over more than a dozen years were largely successful from a profitability perspective, while unquestionably representing super fuel for Toyota, which ranked #9 on the 2019 Forbes Most Valuable Brands listing.[9]

In many ways, Scion was a marketing experiment, and through its auspices, future generations of leaders for Toyota and Lexus were forged, in partnership with ATTIK.

So, drawing from keen observation – as in the case of Elise Mitchell – and through hands-on learning with ATTIK, David C. Baker, Blair Enns, and others, here are my top seven recommendations for you as scaling your business becomes an important objective. To succeed, plan wisely.

1. First, make reasonably sure you can scale profitably: You can only spend money once.
2. Run your business like you are going to franchise it, by documenting all aspects of management and operations effectively enough that others can fully duplicate your success with a minimal amount of training.[10]
3. Understand where you fall on the Greiner Curve and diligently persevere until you reach the next level, or until maximization of your current level is unquestionable.
4. Leverage insights from the likes of Elise Mitchell emphasizing the importance of building and maintaining a brand culture.
5. Drawing upon the language and lessons of design thinking, institutionalize the harvesting of your operation's exploitation, the continuation of its exploration, and unite their lessons on an ongoing basis, to build and sustain success.
6. Prioritize positive customer experiences (CX) and maintain a daily commitment to proactive, intelligent business and professional development.
7. Heed advice ATTIK's partners shared in "Noise Five": Authentic positioning is a matter of life and death, as misrepresentation can lead to ruin.

Exit Strategies and Tactics

Prosper Group is an expert consultancy for PR and marketing communications agencies, specializing in profitability and exit strategies. According to Managing Partner Alex Halbur, "Exit planning includes a plan for the owner, a plan for the organization, a plan for senior talent, and continuity planning. A sub-set of exit planning, succession involves the review of talent and who will replace the CEO, as well as what's going to happen to the various senior roles as that successor steps up."[11]

Mr. Halbur spoke those words during a 2019 appearance on the PR Council's Agencies of the Future podcast, where he also advised owners to give themselves at least five years to prepare themselves and their businesses to transfer ownership. Here is why: If the goal is financial, accurately assessing the firm's value is essential. Developing a deep understanding of the marketplace and the truth about a company's shortcomings is extremely time intensive. Those challenges multiply when the goal is passing ownership over to employees or family members, where the complications are compounded by the changes in leadership, and the many impacts upon all those affected.

Through his extensive writings, Mr. Halbur's suggestions to business owners beginning to plan their exit strategies encourage them to set their goals, account for their resources, and install value drivers, his shorthand for the various business components or functions that raise company values in the eyes of objective buyers. These can include next-level leaders, or even documentation of the company's unique operations.

The 2019 podcast appearance was hosted by Kim Sample, then-president of the PR Council professional association, which represents over 100 PR and communications firms across America and more than 12,000 individuals. Half-way through the interview, Ms. Sample referred to Mr. Halbur's emphasis on key elements of a successful exit – a written plan, time, quantifiable cash flow, and a deep bench of talent – then asked about the ideal agency size for making a sale worthwhile. Mr. Halbur began: "To get meaningful money, you have to have some scale. I would say at least 15-plus employees, and a good profit margin. So, $3-million agency revenues, assuming they have a successor who can maintain that revenue level or grow it."

For the years 2009–2020, DWA billed just over U.S. $194,000, on average. With that perspective, you can see why I am highlighting others' examples in this discussion. To be in the position to cash-in on my company's legacy, I would have to take on a great deal of highly specialized, ambitious, and rigorous work. A venture like Prosper Group is an invaluable resource for pursuing such a monumental objective. If you choose this path, be sure to look for proven experience helping agency owners strategically plan for and manage the sale and/or succession of their businesses.

This brings me back to David C. Baker of ReCourses, Inc. His informed succession-planning counsel makes this excellent point: "Succession planning is one of those very few processes that both carries no downside and also is beneficial no matter what the future holds," he writes. "For example, if you consider succession when making decisions about people, products, and processes, you will enjoy the experience of running the firm even more—regardless of the outcome."[12]

Like Prosper Group, Mr. Baker is a professional guide who can lead you through succession planning to help prepare for your personal future, and for what is to come for your business. That normally includes the in-depth exploration of Valuation, which is also addressed in Mr. Baker's annual one-day intensive workshop entitled "Valuation + Succession for the Modern Marketing Firm." In the event's description, teaching attendees how to run a firm in ways that heighten success for them and their clients is high on the agenda. Thinking that the highest level of effectiveness for my firm requires a commitment to the possibilities of succession, and to the nuts-and-bolts of valuation, is a sort of epiphany for me. Clearly, these are essential factors in business that also apply to the entrepreneurs we serve, and their respective operations. Understanding the nuances of a firm's financial and operational big pictures is a superpower we can surely attain – and wield on our own behalf, as business owners.

As a beacon of leadership education, Elise Mitchell continues to shine. If you are lucky, you may be able to attend one of her workshops focused on the Next Level (see https://www.leadingatthenextlevel.com). In a video promoting these events, Ms. Mitchell reminds us that growing and fulfilling our potential is a journey. With this mindset, referring once again to the U.S. Army's actualization mantra and all the other provocative wisdom illuminated, the arduous notion of scaling one's business can shapeshift into embracing our rights to life, liberty, and the pursuit of happiness. Arriving on this mountaintop of knowledge, I hope one or more of these pathways will help you reach for and achieve your own highest level.

Exploration

1. Explain why succession planning is worth undertaking even if the owner never envisions selling the company or transferring its ownership.
2. Describe valuation, and how it can be affected through a succession transition and eventual sale.
3. Name three ways the addition of a business partner can raise the value of a business.
4. Describe a scenario where a sole proprietorship adds an employee to boost its profitability. In your opinion, what should the skills of that person be, and the scope of their responsibilities?
5. How much money does your consultancy need to bill on a month-to-month basis to be profitable? How does that change when you add one employee, or two?

6. Briefly explain the expectations you had for your business 10 years ago … then imagine the business 10 years from now, and assess its future strengths, weaknesses, opportunities, and threats.
7. Knowing the importance of customer service for your business, how can you build-out your company to maximize marketplace opportunities and operational efficiencies?
8. Knowing the importance of business development, is there some "on-brand" internal effort you can mount to stimulate internal growth while also creating attractive content (like ATTIK's Noise)?
9. What is your plan for selling your business or transferring its ownership? What do you need to do to put the wheels in motion for that transition? What will happen tomorrow if you can no longer work?
10. If you could successfully grow and sell your consultancy, what would you do with your life? Are there things you can do now or in days, weeks, or years to come to prepare yourself for that possibility? Make a plan!

Notes

1 Gallup, Inc. (2020, December 2). What Are the 34 CliftonStrengths Themes? | EN – Gallup. Gallup.Com. http://bit.ly/CStrengths34
2 What is the DiSC assessment? (n.d.). Discprofile.com. Retrieved May 31, 2021, from https://www.discprofile.com/what-is-disc
3 Faw, L. (2019, September 5). MAD: Broadhead Acquires Kohnstamm Communications. MediaPost. http://bit.ly/KC2B2019
4 TED. (2014, June 3). The Psychology of Your Future Self | Dan Gilbert [Video]. YouTube. https://youtu.be/XNbaR54Gpj4
5 Kim, J. (2019, August 29). When do You Really Become Yourself? Psychology Today. http://bit.ly/BUtoday
6 Wikipedia contributors. (2021, April 16). Self-Actualization. Wikipedia. https://en.wikipedia.org/wiki/Self-actualization
7 Mitchell, E. (2016). Leading through the Turn: How a Journey Mindset Can Help Leaders Find Success and Significance (1st ed.). McGraw-Hill Education.
8 Noise Five. (2009). ATTIK.
9 Toyota Motor. (n.d.). Forbes. Retrieved May 31, 2021, from https://www.forbes.com/companies/toyota-motor/
10 Enns, B. (2019, June 12). Why Creative Firms Don't (Really) Scale. Win Without Pitching. http://bit.ly/wwpNoSc
11 The PR Council. (2019, July 2). Episode 14: Planning your Exit Strategy – Things to Consider Five Years Out with Alex Halbur of Prosper Group. PR Council. http://bit.ly/AOFep14
12 Baker, D. C. Succession Overview. http://bit.ly/SuccOvw

Part III
PR Master Toolset

Topics Covered

The Right Marketing Plan 133
Action Plans 142
The Art and Craft of Presentation 152

9
The Right Marketing Plan

Having mastered each of the preceding sections by completing their respective Explorations, you are now fully prepared to be build your career as a communications consultant, and to make measurable impacts for those you serve. The pages to come represent both a summary recap and a chance to investigate some essentials of our field in more depth.

Let's begin calibrating our consulting sights by recalling the ways I encouraged you to be like ATTIK.

- Work hard to prove you can produce something original that is interesting.
- Demonstrate your desire to apply your skill set to others' benefit by engaging with those you can attract and endeavoring to collaborate, professionally.
- Stick with it until the project bears fruit, then use all your energy to celebrate and feature that fruition in ways that tout your contributions strategically.
- Treat your own venture as something great, even in the early going.
- To gain attention, do what you must, making your beliefs evident, and presenting yourself and your offerings authentically and consistently.

Heeding this counsel, you will have a brand that can earn respect among the business gatekeepers you encounter who need your skills. Remember also that your understanding of the continuous customer journey, business development, strategy, and other bedrock tenets of business success – including project management – positions you to focus on the right tactics to serve the most important objectives strategically, starting right away. You have also been introduced to deep-level strategic planning methodologies, like communications audits and marketing plans, which provide strong foundations

DOI: 10.4324/9781003177913-14

for vital marketing initiatives ranging from designing and executing integrated marketing campaigns to handling shrewd, intelligent social media activities.

You have learned to appreciate the world's Alpha companies and their winning internal communications strategies … as well as the ideals of external communications, where all channels are aligned, brands' missions, key messaging, values, and authentic truths culminate, amidst constant evidence of why and how the company matters to its target audiences. Another of the many powerful concepts you own is the <u>organizing idea</u>, which unifies strategy and purpose with a company's essential functions in serving its customers and their needs. By cross-pollinating organizing ideas with promotions-oriented public relations (PR) and media-relations strategy, you can produce extremely valuable media exposure, while also driving mission critical ROI via savvy integrated content marketing.

To win in our role, it is incumbent upon us to make a company's communications with others effective and interesting for its customers – while serving that company's bottom-line objectives strategically. Here is the formula for success: Approach communications from the perspective of doing what is right (i.e., reflecting solid business leadership and management), and being endlessly creative and strategic, the diligent application of brand development science leads us to create information, materials, and content we can use to build meaningful relationships with clients, customers, and new friends.

I hope the tone of this survey reflects your own confidence in your expanding knowledge and capabilities. If not, consider revisiting this book's companion The Communications Consultant's Foundation, and/or recommitting to both books' Explorations. The next objective is increasing our expertise with some of the biggest challenges you will face, sooner or later.

Marketing Plans

The word "plan" is laced throughout this curriculum, underscoring my dedication to preparation. To provide more perspective, when I first saw the opening words of John Rampton's instructive Entrepreneur Magazine article stating the necessity of a documented business plan for every business, my gut response was wholehearted agreement.[1] The truth is this, however, that no such thing exists for my business, and I have not seen one for any of my clients in recent history.

Depending upon your clients' objectives and their willingness to engage in due diligence, creating a full business plan may represent the best-advised starting point, especially if it is a start-up, and/or there is emphasis on investor relations. In those cases, Mr. Rampton's article will serve you very well. I am accustomed to joining forces with businesses that are already going concerns, where things have proceeded well enough for them to start to think about increasing their marketing expertise, if those developments can be justified. As such, for companies seeking to engage a communications or PR consultant, focusing-in on marketing (especially where it supports sales) is usually deemed mission critical.

The Needs Analysis included in Chapter 1 lists ten questions, including one pertaining to prospects' primary marketing objectives, and another specific to their marketing plans. In my experience, while there usually is some clarity on objectives, formal plans are surprisingly rare. Regardless, it is obviously imperative for the communications consultant to inquire about those details, and to absorb the feedback. Any information identified through the process of completing a Needs Analysis forms the basis of your working agenda, pointing you either toward <u>formal</u> communications planning, or its alternative, fire-drill version.

While Needs Analyses are typically conducted prior to being hired, using these five campaign planning steps from the proposal's cover letter, you can begin formulating a marketing plan.

- Step One: Revisit positioning and ensure it is as strong as possible for the foreseeable future.
- Step Two: Identify key business objectives to be served through the PR campaign in the early going, and perhaps second-tier ones to be addressed down the road.
- Step Three: Inventory the company's branding and its owned media channels and discuss how those can be strengthened and used in unison to address its objectives.
- Step Four: Inventory "news-worthy" developments and plan how and when to use those – with the goal of establishing a content calendar for the immediate future or longer term.
- Step Five: Additional planning to support prioritized objectives – for example, media relations, awards, speaking engagements, recruiting, business development, social media, etc.

When you deem the conditions right for beginning work on a marketing plan, I recommend reviewing brand management and marketing expert and author Brad VanAuken's insightful article "Anatomy of a Marketing Plan,"[2] due to its soundness and simplicity. It is easy to become overwhelmed by this challenge, and Mr. VanAuken's recipe is spot-on. He describes the plan as a request for funds, and in the big picture of a business, that is an excellent point: These activities cost time and money, and the plan must promise valuable returns in due course.

While the five campaign planning steps do put you in position to leap right into action, the more expanded investigations and analyses prescribed by many experts are well worth heeding. I have recounted my experience working with PostWorks New York, which began with the preparation of a strategic marketing plan. What I learned and shared through that process prepared me to be especially impactful, versus where I would have been in the fire-drill scenario. That situation was educational for me, and it is something I have sought to repeat under the right conditions. However, I have also learned that sometimes it is necessary to begin with a fire-drill … then to look for the opportunity to flesh-out something more comprehensive when the time is right, after trust has been established.

For further enlightenment, I encourage you to explore this well-vetted content provided by Entrepreneur Magazine and North Carolina's Small Business and Technology Development Center (SBTDC).

- How to Create a Marketing Plan: http://entm.ag/22byug4
- The Ingredients of a Marketing Plan: http://entm.ag/22c9sh8
- SBTDC Guide to Marketing Research (includes downloadable marketing plan worksheet): http://bit.ly/MPstudy

Back to my strategic marketing plan for PostWorks – in order of appearance, these are the sections I included: Introduction; Market Analysis (Target Market; What Offerings Need Marketed to What Customers?); Competitive Analysis; Marketing Strategies (Objectives; Marketing Strategy); Product/Service Analyses; Campaigns (Brand Management; Messaging; Sales; Customer Service; Promotions; Advertising; Public Relations); Call to Action.

From the Entrepreneur Magazine articles and Mr. VanAuken's suggested ingredients, you will notice some missing from this PostWorks plan. Namely, the latter includes no financial records nor projections, nor any costs for marketing expenditures. So how does it provide value when it does not request funds? The answer is this: by getting everyone on the same page strategically and aligning messaging cohesively around the brand and its priorities … bringing order and mindfulness to bear on activities, most of which were already happening. In other words, that version of strategic planning homed in on <u>why</u> and <u>how</u> marketing activities were carried out, and the refinements were deeply impactful.

Relevant to this discussion, I once had a semi-magical encounter with a unicorn. I use this metaphor to mask the individual's identity, and in honor of the situation's rarity and mythological aspects. Bringing it down to Earth, I was interviewed by a prospect who was very advanced in her field, who commanded a venture on track to bill tens of millions of U.S. dollars that year, who shared a short and powerful marketing plan that was highly illuminating. Beginning with Vision and Mission, these sections followed: Positioning and Client Value Proposition; Core Marketing Objectives by Revenue and by Brand Perception/Client Awareness; Marketing Strategies; Marketing Tactics.

That's it. Reading it, I had a very clear sense of this venture's <u>why</u> and its <u>how</u>. While I feel you cannot go wrong by following Entrepreneur Magazine's and Mr. VanAuken's guidance for building marketing plans, substantiating the <u>why</u>, orchestrating the <u>how</u> – and communicating these imperatives to management – may represent marketing planning success for any given client.

Through diligence, I have learned that there is yet another way to distill the type of guiding marketing roadmap shared in my surreal interview: It comes from applying the Kaplan and Norton balanced scorecard approach to marketing.[3] Here is a link to a more in-depth discussion of Kaplan and Norton's balanced scorecard, where you can also download a template to help you translate mission and vision into suitable actions.

- Balanced Scorecard: https://www.toolshero.com/strategy/balanced-scorecard/

Following the authors' lead, practitioners are instructed to start with their Vision and Mission statements. The reference provided is extremely helpful for getting going. Still, I found that process of distilling objectives from four different points of view (financial, customer, internal processes and organizational growth) to be tedious and lifeless … until I learned about the activating ingredient that article leaves out. Thanks to consultant and author Brett Knowles, I learned about Strategy Maps[4] … and you can, too, right here: http://bit.ly/StrtMp.

That video and accompanying article were created for management knowledge platform 12manage.com.[5] In the story, a strategy map is defined as the balanced scorecard framework component illustrating strategies for value creation. "Strategy maps are diagrams that describe how an organization can create value by connecting strategic objectives in explicit cause-and-effect relationship with each other, via the four balanced scorecard perspectives: financial, customer, processes, learning and growth."

Through his presentation, Mr. Knowles details a historic balanced scorecard framework for Southwest Airlines, through to the point of sharing the resulting strategy map is shown in the Figure 6.

These references all lead back to Kaplan and Norton's books, including one entitled <u>Strategy Maps</u>. What I am sharing is just the tip of the iceberg. By watching Mr. Knowles' presentation, you will learn that he has built his successful career by educating himself and his clients on the balanced scorecard

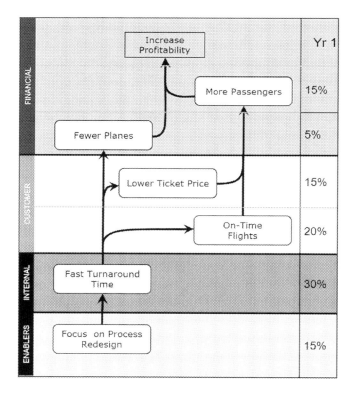

Figure 6: Southwest Airlines Strategy Map[6]
Source: Knowles, Brett, Southwest Airlines Strategy Map, Hirebook.com

principles, and then breaking new ground in their exploration and application. His insights on the benefits of strategy maps are therefore highly valid. Following the ability to monitor performance, he also lists the ability to communicate strategic direction and priorities to all stakeholders, the ability to translate strategy into action that allows everyone to understand their contribution and aligning the organization. These vital attributes of well-managed companies have come to light throughout this book, and I hope you appreciate the power of this analytical approach to organizational optimization.

I suspect this strategic management system was well known to my mythical interview subject. The Southwest Airlines example also appears in The Management Centre's introduction to strategy maps and the balanced scorecard in charities – where it is part of a meticulously detailed and information-rich presentation.[7] The process of deciphering the merits of this treasure trove of knowledge, and translating it into effective action for clients, represents promising opportunities for us all.

Ignition

Arriving at this crossroads between research and action, you may find this query from professional ghost blogger Lacy Boggs helpful: "So what does being a leader with your marketing actually look like? It means looking at all the pieces that are available to you — webinars, videos, podcasts, challenges, blog posts, emails, guest posts, interviews, etc. — and putting them together in a unique way that will best appeal to your ideal customers and your audience."[8]

Put simply, if you are appealing to your customers and your audience, all good business things will follow. If you thoroughly understand the why and can sell-in your plans for how to go about marketing a business, you can aim toward the top objective on your strategy map today (often, profitability) ... and adjust your bearings tomorrow, as necessary.

This marketing era is increasingly fixated on data – a phenomenon which offers deeper understanding of audiences and new opportunities to create relevance. Forrester Research connected this paradigm shift to marketing tactics more than a decade ago, foreseeing the extinction of agencies unable to switch from push to pull marketing, along with any other service-based firm incapable of offering strategy expertise, managing and analyzing data, measuring, and harnessing social media.[9]

Build your marketing plans on insights like these and expect to move the needles in the right directions. If you have the time, budget, and authority to approach it with ample due diligence, the tools mentioned here should improve your aim. On the other hand, if you must leap into action right away, begin your hunt with the campaign planning steps, remember your commitment to constant improvement and the continuous customer journey, and make the biggest impact you can every day.

Exploration

1. Why is it important to have your personal or your business brand fortified as you enter a dialogue with client executives about marketing?
2. Chapter 1 mentions several examples of communications audits. List three benefits of conducting a communications audit, as well as workarounds for generating each of those benefits if you do not have the time to conduct an extensive one.
3. Briefly, how would you aim to make a company's communications with others effective and interesting for its customers – while serving the company's bottom-line objectives strategically?
4. Does every business need to have a written business plan? If so, work on yours. If not, explain your rationale for not needing one.
5. Use the five campaign planning steps to create a strategic marketing plan for your consultancy. Explain the length of time you expect your plan to cover, and when you feel it should be updated.
6. Conduct a simple balanced scorecard assessment for your business.
7. Create a strategy map for your business and list the benefits it provides for you.
8. Describe the difference between a strategic marketing plan based on a fire-drill approach, versus one based on the balanced scorecard management system, with at least five specific distinctions.
9. Provide three examples of what success looks like when a marketing plan is effective, and three more describing situations or developments that reflect a poor marketing plan.
10. What is the best way to convince a client that it is worthwhile to invest into due-diligence and the creation of a marketing plan to strategically unify their marketing operations?

Notes

1 Rampton, J. (2019, February 19). 7 Steps to a Perfectly Written Business Plan. *Entrepreneur.* http://entm.ag/2bHCeXA
2 VanAuken, B. (2021, April 27). Anatomy of a Marketing Plan. Branding Strategy Source. http://bit.ly/AnatMP

3 Kaplan, R. S., & Norton, D. P. (1992, January 1). The Balanced Scorecard – Measures that Drive Performance. *Harvard Business Review*. http://bit.ly/KNmeasure
4 Knowles, B. "Strategy Mapping Overview," YouTube, December 10, 2013, http://bit.ly/StrtMp
5 Strategy Maps (Kaplan Norton). 12manage.com, http://bit.ly/12mSMaps
6 Illustration: Knowles, B. (2013b, December 10). Strategy Mapping Overview [Video]. YouTube. http://bit.ly/StrtMp
7 The Management Centre. (2017, May 22). An Introduction to Strategy Maps and the BSC in Charities. Managementcentre.co.uk. http://bit.ly/BSC_in_C
8 Boggs, L. (2019, October 3). Are You Leading or Following with Your Marketing? Lacy Boggs. https://lacyboggs.com/leading-or-following-with-marketing/
9 Forrester Research, Inc. (2009, July 6). US Interactive Marketing Forecast, 2009 To 2014. Forrester.com. http://bit.ly/IMFus914

10
Action Plans

Everything I had learned in my life up to age 32 was called into play when the leaders of Crest National in Hollywood hired me as their Public Relations (PR) and marketing executive. This was before I had worked at The Terpin Group, where the best practices of PR were applied every day. Crest was the first place where I was responsible for identifying and developing stories to address the express goal of earning media coverage, supported by a substantial marketing budget. Directly interfacing with the media on behalf of a client was also on my plate for the first time ever. Looking back, I feel especially proud of my ability to survey the business environment and focus-in on activities that proved my value. Going in, I never expected it would fall to me to establish sponsorships with major film festivals, or to create the company's website. In many ways, my approach simply involved showing up and getting to work. Giving credit where it is due, my boss John Walker ran a tight ship, and whatever I achieved there was done under his astute guidance and with his support.

As you take the communications consulting torch and run with it, you may pursue full-time employment or you may aim to land clients to serve on a freelance basis. Bear in mind, if you do not go to work in your client's office, it is even more challenging to survey the environment and determine the priorities. Making yourself indispensable, therefore, requires you to hone your own "best practices," to ensure you are always thinking strategically and acting astutely, even when your first-hand knowledge of your client's operations is limited.

I learned a ton from Robert Greene's phenomenal book, "Mastery." One of his major points is this: Our human brains are wonders of the universe that afford us truly extraordinary powers.[1] Whatever position you find yourself in professionally by following your instincts and this instruction, success will

DOI: 10.4324/9781003177913-15

rely on your ability to use your marvelous mind to ensure you are addressing the most important factors. My processes for analyzing client needs, and for intelligently moving forward in addressing them systematically, are already yours. Here are a few more helpful aids.

Objectives and Key Results

Prior to this chapter, we dove into Business and Marketing Plans, examining some of the most scientifically sound approaches for organizing those types of efforts to be efficacious. My constant reminders of the need to be ready to leap into action in short order – addressing the oft-encountered fire-drill scenario – draws directly from my practical experience: So often in my work, when starting out, the orders simply have to do with handling tasks.

Across industries, employees typically want to know what is expected of them, why their work is necessary, and how they are performing. There are two key aspects of your role as a communications consultant that result in heightened pressure: (1) usually, you are not an employee; and (2) you are attempting to help drive high-level marketing programs requiring comprehensive knowledge of a business's current standing.

With this as your plight, simple task completion is probably not going to lead to very much job security. To increase the chances of making yourself indispensable, once again, you will need to employ strategic thinking. For that reason, I am pointing you toward another realm of management science, known as Objectives and Key Results (OKRs). Reportedly, the OKR system has been used at Google for more than 20 years. Consultant and author Brett Knowles has an insightful introductory video[2] for this subject as well: http://bit.ly/OKRpr1. This one uses the following slide (Figure 7).

Coming from the person who has built a career on the formula of Objectives-Strategies-Results, it is clear how this OKR body of knowledge is instrumental for any strategic thinker attempting to ensure that fulfillment of a task is going to be fundamentally sound.

Assessing the best course of action for your future in any assignment is certainly a complicated test. Obviously, when given a task to complete, asking questions may be impractical. This frustrating reality helps to justify the rationale for studying important issues like leadership and management, and even the nuances of how one's role can vary according to the needs of companies of different sizes or characters. Shrewdly taking your soundings to

144 PR Master Toolset

What are Objectives and Key Results?

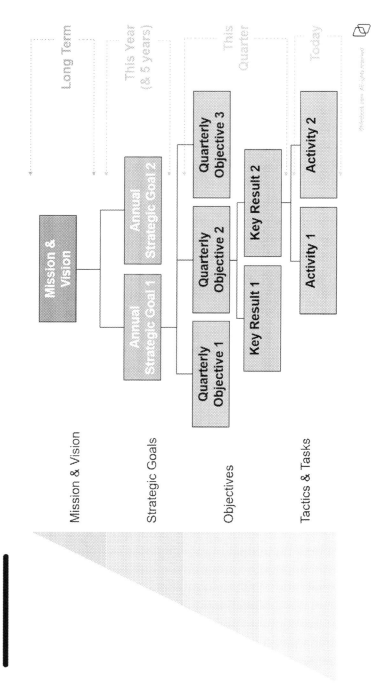

Figure 7: What Are Objectives and Key Results?
Source: Knowles, Brett. Hirebook.com

gain an understanding of a company's mission and vision, and its strategic goals, will help you map out the connections between tasks, the desired key results to come from their completion, and how those activities can affect the company's top line.

This is a simple introduction to OKRs, and further study is highly recommended. However, even taking this basic information to heart has the potential for turning dead-end assignments into chances to demonstrate your ability to use time, expertise, and effort to create meaningful value.

Strategic Plans of Action

Finding our way from facing tactics and tasks we might be assigned to perform to knowing how those will impact an organization's success leads us back to a Marketing Plan ... or perhaps, more specifically, what I call a Marketing Action Plan (MAP). Chapter 9 made the case for the staples of business planning. What I have established for my own needs over time is a streamlined, actionable set of tools that allows me to move forward with confidence, and if the situation requires, support the creation of a meaningful report.

Stepping back from the tedium of arriving at a desk, receiving orders, and attempting to divine the grand order of a client's or employer's business scheme, look again at these Explorations presented at the end of the chapter on Professional Development. Note that these are your own tasks – designed to lead to communications consulting success for you and your superiors, when pursued consistently, day by day.

- Improve your ability to generate targeted media exposure for your clients.
- Improve your ability to build relationships with media professionals and influencers.
- Improve your ability to pitch stories to the media.
- Improve your ability to promote your clients.
- Improve the service you provide to your clients.
- Improve your clients' understanding of the ways PR complements and heightens all other aspects of their marketing.
- Maximize the results and ROI of your campaign efforts for your clients.

With this fastidious, industrious approach to constantly developing your ability to make a positive impact, imagine immersing yourself in all the notes you have gathered by the time you have won an account. In this vision, include all the information brought to light through your Needs Analysis, and by conducting the campaign planning steps. By turning that mountain of data into a list, adding key details on timeline, contacts, and any other proposed plans of action – and then prioritizing the items – you have what I refer to as a PR agenda. Sharing this with your client, weighing in any feedback received and working on completing those agenda items should represent your primary pathway to success.

As time passes, progress occurs, and new information comes to light, updating that PR Agenda for your and your client's reference keeps the progress moving forward.

Let's pause here to consider the client's PR budget, which determines how much time you have available over a course of weeks. If you have a budget of $1,000 for a month and you are charging $100 per hour, you might be in trouble if you use all 10 hours in your first week. Clearly, determining the best course of action on behalf of a client on any given day is based on the status of (1) the PR Agenda, (2) the budget, and (3) your understanding of a client's preference for locking versus flexing its budget to accommodate your efforts. This is where your timekeeping efforts become mission critical.

For my business, I have built spreadsheets that show me the PR Agenda along with the number of hours remaining in the current period, relative to each client. I also enter notes to estimate the amount of time the different agenda items may require in the current period, or others to come.

Whenever I have ample time to plan beyond managing the top-most agenda items, I will create what I call a Client Journal. This document lists out the items from the PR Agenda, but also adds notes on article ideas, client wishes, business developments, or anything else relevant to the company's communications. I also use this document – which is typically printed and kept readily available – to list the top media targets for that company. Any research on upcoming editorial or speaking opportunities is also included, with dates for further action. These journals create powerful, momentous summations, and put me in excellent position to quickly understand the main activities requiring my proactive diligence. Even outdated journals can be useful for quickly surmising past planning efforts, and to home in on important editorial opportunities that may reoccur.

With up-to-date knowledge of a client's budget status, a PR Agenda and a Client Journal often represent everything I need to ensure I am on the right track in putting my key skill set to work on their behalf. Remember, that ensemble of complementary disciplines includes Account Management, Customer Service, Planning, Writing, Media Relations, Measurement, and Reporting.

I have mentioned the luxury of having ample time for planning and made a case for why it is well advised to take aim before firing. Even when you are pressed for time, explaining your ideas to your client contacts is key to winning their support and engagement. For these reasons, it is wise to consider the creation of a MAP. Not only will a MAP guide you in all the practices described above, but it will also increase the chances of delivering key results.

When shared with your client, this document is also likely to build confidence in your tactics and methodologies among upper management, the value of which cannot be overstated. On the other hand, if the response from the company's leaders is critical, you then have the chance to gather and address their input in an updated MAP, which is yet another opportunity to strengthen your role moving forward.

To be clear, a MAP is a report you prepare to be shared with your clients, with these goals: demonstrating your nuanced understanding of the company and its objectives; summarizing the information and processes you will use to generate key results; and illuminating some of the known marketing opportunities coming up soon.

Traditionally, my MAPs have these headings: Marketing Mission; Key Messages and Objectives; Marketing Content (Boilerplate; Electronic Press Kit; Story Pitches; Press Releases); Industry Events; News Coverage; Feature Coverage; Advertising and Event Sponsorship; Executive Positioning; Selected Editorial Opportunities. Each time I have created such a document, the client engagement has extended exponentially (Table 7).

Always remember Robert Greene's counsel encouraging reliance on your mental faculties. In any setting where you have been briefed and are plotting a course of action, you are aiming to provide communications expertise to those you may not yet understand completely. Still, consider this lesson from my experiences: Despite spending nearly every hour of client service in my own office, on average, my business relationships last for several years. I attribute this to listening, researching, and making educated guesses about my clients' inner workings (what I often call "seeing around corners"). Also, to this point, I feel the regular weekly practice of journaling holds great power. To clarify, there are Client Journals described in this chapter; what I am referring to here is more of an agency journal or diary, which is typically just a weekly, unstructured outpouring of thoughts related to my clients from my own perspective.

Table 7: Client Activity Organizer

Check/update electronic press kit (EPK) sites
Track media and update EPK site "In the News" listings
Create media/action plans for known/upcoming projects
Update client journals
Identify/schedule editorial calendar submissions
Handle editorial calendar/"Help A Reporter Out" (HARO) pitches
Develop/pursue feature story opportunities
Manage social media accounts
Handle strategic seeding activities
Research awards info and deadlines, and contribute to submissions
Submit work to relevant directory or trade association sites
Create case studies, submit them to directory/trade association sites, and/or share using social media
Author/post/promote blog postings
Create marketing plans
Identify prime media targets for editorial calendar and advertising research and connect with ad reps

As I have written before, I am adamant about documenting business relationships for one's own benefit. I also write multi-page journal entries at least once a week, where I usually have a brief entry for each active client, and others I am in touch with for business purposes. By cross-referencing this documentation, I am always able to study the arc of any given relationship quite effectively, depending upon how much nuance and detail I have recorded.

Over time, this practice has proven invaluable in diagnosing problems (whether for my clients or for my own business), and in prescribing treatments. Those treatments may result in me simply updating a PR Agenda and getting busy fulfilling those tasks; or embarking on a more exhaustive effort to substantiate and communicate a PR campaign in the form of a MAP. Alternatively, my analysis may lead me to undertake a larger mission – perhaps a Strategic Marketing Plan, a Marketing Plan, or a Business Plan – a smaller one (a critical task), or something in-between (a Client Journal entry).

Action Plans 149

Focus

There is one question you must face-down constantly in your role as a communications consultant: Considering your objectives and the resources you must work with, what is your best move? By using the toolset and practices described here, and conducting your due diligence, I expect you will find that very often, the answers present themselves. Whenever they do not – dig deeper. Immerse yourself within the Balanced Scorecard methodology and see it through by creating a Strategy Map; perform an OKR assessment to identify Key Results to aim for soon, and based on your understanding of essential business imperatives, propose a communications strategy that will positively impact the operation, the human resources, the customers, and the bottom line (Figure 8).

If business is good, champion the stories and the people who are making it so. If prospects pale, you have the skills to lead the turnaround. Taking Darnell's Law to heart (every new development, good or bad, is half challenge and half opportunity), you understand the need to stay on your toes, to be ready to prove yourself each moment of every day. Your commitment to extraordinary customer service will take you extremely far ... and by sharpening your communications expertise and advancing it on behalf of your clients, doing your homework and reaching for the stars, the results are sure to be spectacular.

Exploration

1. As a communications consultant or professional, how do you structure your first day on the job to begin earning your keep as quickly as possible?
2. You are assigned the task of creating a promotional product for the sales team to use as a leave-behind item. Describe your process for determining the objectives behind it and ensuring the end-product delivers key results.
3. I always make a point of telling my client company liaison (or my boss) that a big part of my job is making him/her look good. Do you agree this is a sound strategy? Why or why not?
4. When being given an assignment, asking too many questions can be impractical. Describe three scenarios involving a company's marketing activities when failing to ask questions before beginning work can be disastrous.
5. While a liaison or an organization may not appear to support in-depth marketing planning, sound strategic planning can be educational. Review the list of MAP headings provided and estimate how much time

150   PR Master Toolset

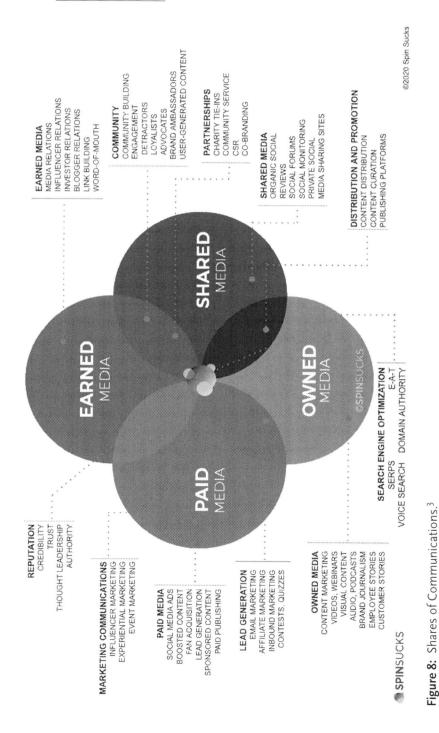

Figure 8: Shares of Communications.[3]

Source: Dietrich, G. (2020, October 7). PESO Model: Does Paid Media Belong with Communications? Spin Sucks. http://bit.ly/2rgoSb4

it might take to summarize that type of content for a client company. For practice, consider creating a MAP for your own consultancy, or for a pro-bono client.
6. My regular prescription for job performance excellence includes diligent professional development, PR agenda management and focus, writing a weekly agency journal, and keeping in close contact with my key client points of contact. How can you adapt these practices to benefit your career progress, starting today?
7. In my business model, the need to accurately track and report time usage is imperative. Devise and describe your system for tracking your time and reporting it for billing purposes and start using it today. My monthly billing projection calls for 40 hours to be spent serving my own agency. How much time should you spend building and supporting your own company and in developing yourself professionally?
8. You have used up your client's budget for the month and you have some important work to do before the next period starts. Options include: (1) stop work until the next period; (2) ask for an overage budget; and (3) ask to begin using the next period's budget now, with the goal of stretching it as far as possible. Which option is best, and how do you resolve the situation with your client?
9. Based on the Client Journal I have described, create one for your consultancy or for a pro-bono client. To ensure the information is as effective as possible for your day-to-day usage, when should you plan to update this document again?
10. A potential client calls you out-of-the-blue with a short-term assignment demanding immediate attention. If you choose to pursue the project (versus providing a proposal and getting a signed letter agreement), how can you structure the deal to sort fair compensation, but also communicate your proposed action plan? (Hint, consider getting your client to agree to your hourly rate, billing in advance (perhaps $1,000 increments) and requesting immediate payment, with "creating an Action Plan" as the first order of business, once you are on the clock).

Notes

1 Greene, R. (2013). Mastery (Reprint ed.). Penguin Books.
2 Illustration: Knowles, B. (2016, March 28). A Practical OKR Primer [Video]. YouTube. http://bit.ly/OKRpr1
3 Illustration: Dietrich, G. (2020, October 7). PESO Model: Does Paid Media Belong with Communications? Spin Sucks. http://bit.ly/2rgosb4

11
The Art and Craft of Presentation

More than 50 years ago, Marshall McLuhan made a series of profound points in his seminal book, *The Medium is the Massage*. Among them, he suggested that the rise of television and folk singing were closing the gap between rationalization and action, radically altering social interaction. Through these insights, he suggested we had returned to our ancestral roots, and were once again living in a village.[1]

Today, most of us are drawn to our screens, large and small. To find the richest storytelling, the most up-to-date information, and almost anything else considered noteworthy or important, if we are not beholding a staged performance, we are usually either staring at some electronic canvas or interacting with speakers to program our desired sounds. In the 1980s, thanks to the release of the Personal Computer (PC) and some innovative software, desktop publishing rapidly began reshaping the world. Allowing anyone with a PC to create original printed matter, it also empowered modern storytellers with vast abilities to create screen content of the highest order. Now, the same iPhones we carry are used to create movies, TV shows, podcasts, and commercials. Clearly, the ability to seize the spotlight at the tribal campfire and captivate the village is in now in almost everyone's hands.

Even when we are stuck in our bedrooms, those moments when we stand up to tell our stories for all to hear are benchmarks of human growth. As we age, learn, and seek to share our knowledge – or influence others – the ability to tell a story effectively is a vital attribute. On the world stage, storytellers who can artfully combine their knowledge with sights, sounds, and other effects conduct magic into audience experiences, affecting their listeners in ways they may never forget.

In academia and in business, as one succeeds, the need to present generally rises. To me, this phenomenon corresponds with the dilemma faced by

DOI: 10.4324/9781003177913-16

business leaders and our companies: To continue to earn and keep followers or customers, we must constantly prove our worth (or "perform"). Otherwise, the battle for attention moves on to other fronts, leaving us behind. While this book largely illuminates the means for providing these proofs, the topic of presentation warrants more attention.

Going back to May 1998, my wife and I had been living in Los Angeles for five months, and I was desperate for employment. Prior to leaving Orlando, I had learned how to network and pursue job opportunities successfully. Surprisingly often, upon seeing something I wanted and sending a cover letter and resume, I would get an interview and win the job. After learning how completely different that story was in LA, finally landing an interview with Crest National's EVP of Sales and Marketing felt miraculous. The third interview ended with me accepting his offer and began an exciting phase of my career.

Until then, I had never put much thought into *positioning* myself as a marketing or PR executive, since my dream job involved being a writer and producer. As I went from being just another job applicant to a contender for Crest's marketing position, I sensed the need to present myself more powerfully, to ensure the company's leaders saw me for all my strengths. To achieve that, I created, printed, bound, and delivered the polished presentation that helped me land the job. Made in PowerPoint, it was entitled, "Roger Darnell's Role in the Future of Crest National."

Two years later, I relaunched Darnell Works, Inc., as The Darnell Works Agency, aiming to provide results-oriented PR support to a short list of phenomenally talented companies, but also to develop and publish original content. The reference to publishing encapsulated pieces I had created that I felt were important, like the Crest National PowerPoint, and various collateral pieces … from DVDs to business cards, invitations, and much more, including websites.

In retrospect, the ability to create and publish professional-looking documents and screen presentations relies upon a skill set that paid immense dividends in my work for Crest National, and subsequently, with The Spark Factory, The Terpin Group, and the clients of The Darnell Works Agency. Reviewing what I have referred to as the communications consultant's key skill set (Account Management, Customer Service, Planning, Writing, Media Relations, Measurement, and Reporting), these other capabilities are not mentioned specifically. As such, completing your preparations for success as a communications consultant requires us to advance your proficiency in a few more pivotal areas.

Presentations

Recalling my story about the presentation prepared for the leaders of Crest National, consider how that effort helped me win a job that easily could have gone to someone else. That summary may spark your memories of a successful half-time speech or a poignant TED Talk; in each example, someone decided to make an impact on others, then used words – and perhaps some teaching aids – to influence a crowd.

When it comes to marketing and sales, attention can be difficult to come by. In fact, accessing it for just a few seconds can cost millions of dollars, as proven each year by Super Bowl advertisers. This standing need to gain attention in a chaotic world drives disciplined communicators to focus, and scientifically leverage tried-and-true methods for reaching and moving audiences. Just as singers rely on the strengths of their performances and material, public speakers and sales professionals live or die by the success of their presentations.

To adopt their discipline and begin formulating what we need to say, show, or share to make our points and potentially compel listeners into action, the often-referenced copy platform serves us here as well. Filling it in and following its prescriptions provides the means for developing subject matter strategically, in deference to our audiences. Bear in mind, for many reasons, the effectiveness of PowerPoint as a means of presenting can be limited. Nonetheless, by concentrating on the copy platform's core tenets (objective(s), target audience, etc.) and preparing a talk you deem to be interesting – with an upbeat beginning and middle, and a rousing ending – you can make a compelling case, share your views, and possibly influence the behavior of your listeners.

From my time with Century III through the present, I have seen that almost every company will have some type of website or online presence – as well as a set of "trade media" news and social media outlets where their most important business developments are detailed, dissected, and debriefed. To engage with customers, the best in any given class of business will build and maintain integrated marketing campaigns ... while for others, brochures and business cards remain standard tools of the trade. However, across most types and classes of business, in the trenches where deals are made, the most vital sales tools that educate prospects and lead to purchase typically take the form of a presentation.

1. As one indication of the enduring importance of the TV commercial, the cost of placing a 30-second ad rose to U.S. $5.6 million for 2020s

Super Bowl.[2] That fee is above-and-beyond the cost of producing the commercial and all other aspects of mounting a marketing campaign.
2. For the global film industry, 280 films were released in theaters in 2019, with hundreds more released online.[3] To a large extent, attracting viewers comes down to movie trailers, which today, are meticulously engineered to maximize content and release strategy.[4] Similarly, music videos help drive purchases of music downloads and albums, while game and book trailers are made to give developers and titles the star treatment, to benefit sales.
3. Also, on the subject of book authors – stage presentations and other public speeches often pave the way to book-signing events and sales.
4. In the expanding world of television, networks sell their programs to advertisers in Upfront presentations, then to audiences via integrated campaigns that include promos (where variations include teasers, bumpers, and other branded content snippets).
5. To attract and close advertisers, media outlets offer Media Kits – containing specific information about their coverage, their audience, testimonials, and information buyers need to place ads and prepare them for inclusion. In the field of public relations, we use Press Kits to package key details media professionals need to vet sources, including bios, backgrounders, and press releases.
6. When my creative industry clients successfully attract a prospect, the result is often an invitation to present. A Sales Kit is standard fare for these in-person meetings; they may include a capabilities deck (essentially a slideshow), case studies, company/executive biographies – and probably a treatment prepared in response to a specific Request for Proposal (RFP).
7. While commercials are still widely effective, consumers are increasingly opting out. To address this, the world's most savvy marketers are increasingly embracing experiential marketing to engage consumers by creating experiences they flock toward and happily interact with.[5]

Let's drill a bit further into each of these hard-working types of presentations.

Advertising and Commercials

My first goal in this chapter is getting you to think about taking command of storytelling and presentation opportunities, whether they occur due to a fee being paid or access being granted on some other basis. By their nature, commercial ads have a very well understood existential premise: Their owners create them to influence or drive viewer behavior, and to a large extent, their broadcast appearances require a media buy. Of U.S. $560 billion spent worldwide on advertising in 2019, 40% occurred in the United States., the world's largest ad market, with less than 20% going to China, the second largest market.[6]

Despite broadcast commercial exposure requiring paid placement, massive audiences will eagerly search out certain kinds of commercials by choice. For example, if a spot uses humor extremely effectively, and/or of it achieves fame or notoriety due to its content or placement, it can be sought out and watched repeatedly, leading to permanent standing in the pop culture zeitgeist. Behind the scenes, the models, actors and voice artists, the brand marketers, the agency executives and worker bees, and all those responsible for the many allied crafts represented in the final product (from drawing storyboards to styling hair and makeup) will use the commercial to sell themselves and attract more work. To serve this sprawling ancillary market – which also leverages consumer interest – there are countless trade associations, media outlets, award programs and content streams fed by creators, craftspeople, fans, and other opportunists eager to avail themselves of the broad attention.

When I was a fledgling communications consultant, I had the amazing good fortune of connecting professionally with some of the world's most successful talents making commercials. Among them are Academy Award-winning editor Angus Wall of Rock Paper Scissors and Emmy Award-winning commercial director Erich Joiner. Since 1995, Mr. Joiner's production company Tool of North America has touted its unique expertise by emphasizing its mastery of "very, very short films, with blatant product placement."[7]

To be successful in my PR role, not only have I had to learn how to understand and support a commercial campaign from a brand's point of view, but also from the perspective of ad agencies and all others involved in making and consuming them. With a greater appreciation for what commercials do so effectively, who cares about them, and why, I have been able to help my clients maximize their involvement in this high-profile field for their own marketing purposes.

At the Super Bowl level, brands and their agencies leave little to chance when it comes to communications, and whenever I have a client involved in creating an ad for this platform, it is always time to listen very intently, and to follow others' leads through a game plan that is sure to be nuanced and tightly controlled. While all other placements pale in comparison, the pride of ownership for brands, agencies, directors, and other key collaborators involved can be surprisingly high, even for dog food commercials. Imagining the full spectrum of media outlets serving consumers and trade pros behind-the-scenes details about the newest Nike campaign – and the owned and social channels for all the makers and contributors, combined – there is enough to be said and shown from many prominent commercials to fill the pages of a magazine.

Turning the details from that featured content – the commercial itself – into stories that market the players involved, in ways that are attractive to their target audiences, is a thrilling adventure for people like us. Showcasing the work on owned and social media, developing and promoting case studies, supporting sales by providing input into bios and reels, and helping to gain exposure when projects are new or any time they can be made relevant – this is the fare of the day-to-day PR agenda when serving a company in this space.

For clients operating outside the creative industry, think about all the types of video content being used to promote businesses and causes, and see if you can mount a campaign with assets that are as prolific, engaging, and powerful as a TV commercial. If it is good enough, leveraging behind-the-scenes storytelling may flesh out your to-do list, and result in some phenomenal marketing victories.

Trailers and Music Videos

I love the example of trailers, because their very name reflects the fact that their original usage (created to be shown *after* movies) has changed. Early film exhibitors quickly learned that audiences would not stick around to watch previews of coming attractions after their movie ended, although screenings before the show were willingly endured. Now, as bona-fide proclamations informing fans that certain movies are forthcoming, trailers are mission-critical in entertainment marketing. Due to ongoing revolutions in the media landscape and changing consumer preferences, the trailer field is subject to constant innovation and reinvention.

As also mentioned previously, the game and book publishing industries have co-opted the film industry's means for creating audience-building excitement through audiovisual storytelling: There are now trailers for novels and other book forms, and for videogames.

Back in the movie culture, research from writer, producer and film data researcher Stephen Follows indicates that the average trailer length is around two minutes.[8] The developers of StudioBinder video production software publish an amazingly resourceful blog, where articles include, "How to Make a Movie Trailer that Grabs Attention."[9] That story lists some software that can be used to create trailers: Apple's iMovie and Final Cut, Adobe Premiere, and Avid Media Composer. Indeed, this is the same editorial software used to create commercials and other types of motion picture content. When you want to add 2D or 3D Computer-Generated Imagery (CGI), you will need to explore other packages like Adobe Illustrator and Maxon Cinema 4D (C4D). To add visual effects, use Adobe After Effects. This is just a brief glance into the intensive realm where ideas are cinematically brought to life by skilled artists.

Convincing audiences to watch your movie, read your book, play your videogame, listen to your podcast or perhaps some other activity you wish to attract them to requires a great deal of skill and craftsmanship. That said, as time marches forward, new software solutions are simplifying the complexity. For one example, in 2019, Spotify's Anchor podcasting app added the ability to easily create one-minute trailers.

For the annual Super Bowl broadcasts, recent television audiences have exceeded 100 million viewers.[10] Meanwhile, according to research from Statista, the trailer for "Avengers: End Game" was watched 289 million times in its first day of release.[11] Tapping the storytelling power of the trailer is yet another top tier means for grabbing attention, in the situation where you have something suitably awesome to promote.

Then comes the music industry, and its hallmark contribution to decade-after-decade of televised global pop culture: the music video. I do not know much about Max Wevers, but his YouTube channel has over 800,000 subscribers, and his "top 30 most viewed music videos of all time" is jaw-dropping (https://youtu.be/JLZ9fP2AiTI). Views for each video appearing in his compilation exceed two billion; the top performer exceeds six-and-a-half billion. Unlike the movie trailer, which promotes a feature film, the music video *is* the feature film, despite the length typically being just a few minutes, in alignment with its song. There are also the examples of Michael Jackson and Pharrell Williams, whose pioneering innovations led to a 40-minute video for Mr. Jackson's "Ghosts" in 1997, and the Guinness World Record-holding 24-hour video for Mr. Williams' "Happy" in 2013.[12]

As is the case with television commercials, consumers take interest in how music videos are made, and the ancillary "trade media" market for insider news about this form of artistry is considerable. For those involved, amplifying their work effectively involves diligence across multiple facets – just like those in the commercial space. The consumer-focused and trade-media outlets differ, as do the buyers and clients … but the promotional activities and the importance of credits, reels and "sales reps" are parallel.

The Art and Craft of Presentation

Music videos are known to be instrumental in selling music. This nexus is rich for communications consultants – and its trade tricks are worth stealing and adapting to serve marketing needs in other industries.

Stage Presentations

Before the existence of YouTube and TED Talks, a handful of political and commencement speeches represented the most famous instances of a speaker standing before a crowd and making history. Courtesy of traditional media but also Wikipedia, we know that President Kennedy spoke of going to the moon in Houston in 1962, and that a year later, Martin Luther King Junior shared his heartfelt dream of racial equality in Washington, D.C. Meanwhile, it is a direct attribute of YouTube that millions upon millions of people have watched J.K. Rowling's 2008 commencement speech at Harvard University. As a result of these individuals stepping up to microphones and speaking, generations have been inspired to dream, think, and act.

These days, we all can thank the TED Talks organization, and worldwide interest in the types of uplifting presentations they foster – generally limited to 18 minutes or less – for helping us understand that many people possess the ability to give powerful talks when challenged to be extremely innovative and engaging. While most of us have sat through presentations that bored us to tears, the proliferation of TED Talks and widespread backlash against PowerPoint are introducing some refinements. To avoid the over-use of wordy slides, and thereby increase collaboration and knowledge transfer, author, consultant, and Inc. Magazine columnist Geoffrey James suggests using no slides – or providing audience members with briefing documents or fill-in-the-blank workbooks.[13]

To many of us, PowerPoint and its clones remain extremely useful, if only to organize presentations and rehearse them. The ability to create a handout from the slides is another benefit that can engage audience members long after a talk has ended – or as mentioned in my Crest National anecdote, shore up a communications initiative when an in-person presentation is impossible. To develop a presentation that will make a point for the audience in a memorable way, I encourage the use of any/all means necessary.

Sooner or later, all those aspiring to lead and influence understand they will need to step forward, speak up, rally the troops, and make themselves heard. Start small – perhaps through a local club or gathering – or large, by pitching the organizers of an upcoming business event. Polish your speech and seize the day, building upon the wisdom shared in this book through the likes of

Lars Sudmann and other accomplished speakers, by giving your audiences something valuable to remember.

After several decades of TED Talks, I find it interesting to survey those which have proven to be the most popular. In TED's Top 25 list, the subjects certainly stand out: addressing schools' effects on creativity; the importance of body language; the most effective means of inspiring action; speaking so that people will listen; and sharing little known information about orgasms.[14] I am sure you will also give high marks to each speaker on this list. Study them and follow their examples – and you will go far.

It has been a few years since the remarkable story of Randy Pausch, Ph.D., played out. To summarize, the charismatic, energetic, and wonderfully ambitious Carnegie Mellon University professor received a terminal pancreatic cancer diagnosis in the summer of 2007. That September, he created and delivered a "last lecture" seen and heard around the world (thanks to YouTube), which you can experience here: https://www.cmu.edu/randyslecture.[15] The following April, the book entitled "The Last Lecture," co-written by Jeffrey Zaslow, was published by Hyperion, achieving New York Times bestseller status for 18 months. Dr. Pausch passed away on July 25, 2008.

For each of us, there is so much to learn from viewing this fateful stage presentation, where we can contemplate what it might look like if our lives were ending, and we had the chance to share our wisdom, or whatever story we wished to tell. For Dr. Pausch, the focus was on encouraging his audience to pursue their dreams, while also enabling the dreams of others. All these years later, through his inspired communications efforts, Dr. Pausch is still inspiring people to act according to his wishes. If I am not mistaken, his speech was delivered using PowerPoint slides.

Sales Presentations

In her 2018 article for Activia Training entitled "Why Do We Need Presentation Skills," Ashley Andrews answers the question definitively. According to her, mastering this craft is the difference between winning and losing, and between succeeding and failing.[16]

In the worlds of television, print and online media, if you have an interest in buying advertising, you can rest assured that you will soon confront the most powerful and polished message of strength the seller can muster for you. To satisfy investors, brand leaders prepare and present earnings reports; then, the smartest of them find ways to tease their latest wares for their customers, as Apple does each year on the stage at its Worldwide Developers Conference. To woo brands into a business relationship, agency leaders shape their capabilities decks, featuring case studies and customized pitches to share their visions and strategies, and to propose innovative tactics.

The same is true on down the line: For all those wishing to join the fray on the marketing battlefield, they must prove their worth by presenting themselves and their achievements, masterfully using words, images, video, and sound in artful combinations, which usually play out on screens.

Given consumers' growing interests in having the brands they support embrace purpose and demonstrate meaningful values, branded experiences (which might be described as *performances*) are here to stay as integral aspects of building relationships – and closing sales.

Taking all this information into account, can you doubt the importance of developing and applying presentation skills? The clear pathway forward is exemplified by the late, great Stan Lee, who ended many statements with a patent expression for eternal aspiration: "Excelsior!"

Websites

Introduced in Jay Baer's "Youtility" book, a vignette highlighting River Pools and Spas brilliantly illustrated how the owner changed his business strategy to effectively adopt content marketing, after years of relying on advertising to drive new business. Both Mr. Baer's book and my own "The Communications Consultant's Foundation" provide more bright advice for understanding the nuanced sales and marketing approaches smart people are using to set themselves and their businesses apart.

Among the other bedrock tenets of business success we have explored together are the powers that come from reputation management, strategic brand building, telling stories, and demonstrating values. At all times, there is also the constant battle for attention, and a need to be proactive and interesting to engage audiences. With increasing reliance on mobile phones, and rising digitalization, does it surprise you to learn that a large percentage of small businesses have no website?

Over the past several years, business-to-business ratings and reviews platform Clutch has conducted surveys of small business owners, where in 2018, 36% of them admitted having no website, for these reasons: Website is not relevant to industry (27%); cost (26%); use social media instead (21%); lack technical knowledge (15%).[17] By doing a little research, you can see for yourself that no great cost nor technical knowledge is necessary to build a web presence. Given the way we all assess products and services before we buy them (by researching them online), it is hard to imagine any type of business that would not benefit from even the simplest kind of website.

In this treatise on the importance of presenting ourselves to the world, think about the vital role of a website in validating the credibility of a person or business. Ideally, it is optimized for mobile viewing – and it offers all the key information potential customers need to evaluate the legitimacy of the business and its principals, and to strongly consider making a purchase.

California-based agency owner and Forbes Agency Council member T. Maxwell has written a thoughtful series of articles about digital marketing. In one entitled "The Role of a Website Today," he writes: "Most of what we do in digital marketing, be it SEO, social media, pay-per-click or email marketing, is to drive quality leads to a website and encourage them to complete a form, make a phone call, or make a purchase. That is the end game for most businesses. I always tell our clients that they need to think about their website as the mother ship – it's the most important piece of your digital marketing assets."[18] Simply put, I could not agree more.

Back to the discussion about River Pools and Spas, a trip to the company's website (on a computer, smart TV, or smartphone) is illuminating: https://www.riverpoolsandspas.com. You can rest assured that Mr. Sheridan is continuing to invest in every facet of digital marketing listed by Mr. Maxwell. And for those who wind up on his company's very well-designed mother ship, two calls to action are inescapable: REQUEST PRICING, and Subscribe to the blog now! Additionally, the company's products and principals, its backstory, the feedback of its customers, high quality video presentations ... you will find it all there for everyone to see, 24/7.

When it comes to demonstrating the importance of a website in presenting a business and contributing to its success, in my opinion, this closes the case.

Social Networks

Given his role with the Forbes Agency Council – and his mission to attract high-level clientele to his agency through marketing strategies that are innovative and proven – I am impressed by another of T. Maxwell's articles. On the subject of "The Essence of Social Media and Hospitality," he identifies two things that can be achieved with social media very effectively: attracting new customers and communicating with them on a casual basis. While his example skews toward the particulars of hoteliers, I feel it applies widely: "The goal is to create the cocktail party that everybody wants to come to and nobody wants to leave," he writes, promising, "Direct bookings will follow."[19]

In 2021, I am tending to focus on helping my clients regularly show "signs of life" on four social media networks: Facebook, Instagram, LinkedIn, and Twitter. Given the inevitability of change in this realm of the media, I am regularly surprised about the enduring validity of these networks. When asked about Returns on Investments for social media, there is usually abundant quantitative and qualitative evidence, indicating success or failure. However, I still believe that intelligently using these highly trafficked, easily customized, low-cost outposts to strategically reflect a brand's activity in something close to real time is as necessary as unlocking the front door for a restaurant. Another metaphor I use to describe social media usage is to use channels to compile and present a trophy case of achievements.

We have covered content marketing, social media, and search engine optimization in Chapter 3, and the link provided to Hootsuite's guide to creating a social media content calendar remains golden (http://ow.ly/VSOt30nsh39). Rewards are sure to come from innovation in building and expanding reputations, strengthening brands, taking the stage, and activating core values – but even just communicating these foundational facets consistently will set a brand apart, even if the brand is you personally.

Social media networks will come and go, but with all of us habitually compelled to use one or another every day, and massive fortunes at stake for developers, they are our present and future. Where large groups congregate and can be reached, marketers follow, like predators surrounding a watering hole. For communications consultants, having a working knowledge of the most popular gathering spots is imperative, and being able to use them to build and maintain a presence, strategically, is a higher level of mastery that is bankable.

The Digital and Physical Savant

Search for "top social network sites," and you will find listings with dozens – if not hundreds – of sites, some of which are sure to be new to you. In late 2019, Santa Monica-based company Mediakix appraised the values of Facebook, Instagram, Snapchat, and Twitter; combined, the numbers add up to U.S. $650 billion.[20] Obviously, these vibrant marketplaces offer tremendous wealth to the developers and stakeholders, but also to those with the working knowledge and expertise to wield the networks for marketing purposes.

Mediakix is one of the growing ranks of companies that exist to reach influencers, primarily by building expertise on platforms like Instagram and YouTube, and then leveraging it.

You too can "follow the money" to success, if you can hone your expertise around networks or platforms that are attracting engagement on a large scale, or even within certain niches. Let's say you find affinity between your interests and client demands in the realm of video. Exploring platforms like Facebook, Instagram, Snap, TikTok, Twitch, Twitter, Vimeo, WhatsApp, YouTube, and others, how can you take advantage of their reach and capabilities in your work?

The creation of websites, microsites, blogs, and similar landing pages is also within your grasp. Skills can be attained by learning to code, and/or by exploring Medium, Pinterest, Twitter, Tumblr, WordPress, and countless other platforms in daily use worldwide. Meanwhile, stages and soapboxes live on, and the ability to use one's voice alone – or in tandem with storytelling conventions heightened by music, and/or technologies like motion sensing, reactive graphics, and projection mapping – can move mountains.

Choose well, and by mastering one or more physical and/or digital communications niche, you can become the specialist referred by that platform to help others exploit it. When this vision plays out and your dream comes to life, please drop me a line or give me a call. Moving forward, I would love to be able to learn from your success.

Exploration

1. What are the seven components of the copy platform? I memorized them to pass a test in college, and I strongly suggest you do the same. The acronym is COTSBPA.
2. A potential client asks to see your capabilities deck. What do you do to prepare this and get it in front of her ASAP?
3. When you think about closing a sale for your consultancy, what do you need to include in your sales kit, and how will you present those items as effectively as possible? Be prepared to answer that question accordingly for any company you work for.
4. What is the best approach to address your marketing needs – advertising, content marketing, media relations, or some combination? Knowing how to answer questions like this will make you an invaluable resource – especially when your counsel pays off.

5. Due to the popularity (and effectiveness) of commercials, trailers and music videos, knowledge of these realms can open many doors. Investigate the highest rated videos in these categories at the present, and regularly update your knowledge monthly.
6. Explore the website https://www.pechakucha.com – then see if you can connect with a local group to hear others give PechaKucha presentations, and to share your own.
7. Toastmasters International is a non-profit educational organization that teaches public speaking and leadership skills through a worldwide network of clubs. I encourage you to visit https://www.toastmasters.org to find a local group, attend two meetings, and see where that leads.
8. Pick a high-profile media outlet, visit its website, and look for information on advertising, which should lead you to a Media Kit. Can you find what you need to contact a salesperson, if you wanted to place an ad?
9. Fortunately for me, I have often been paid to learn. The methodologies prescribed in this book can put you in the same position, if you can convince clients you can deliver value. Make the case for why you should be paid to learn something you do not know, like how to use a new social media platform.
10. In the introduction to this book, I asked what you would talk about in your own TED Talk. The time has come for you to choose a subject, outline and rehearse your talk, present it, and ensure it is recorded. Then, market it to the benefit of your career, using everything you have learned.

Notes

1 McLuhan, M., & Fiore, Q. (1967). The Medium is the Massage: An Inventory of Effects (1st ed.). Bantam Books.
2 Poggi, Jeanine, "Who's Buying Ads in Super Bowl 2020," AdAge, December 20, 2019: http://bit.ly/sbliv-ad
3 The-Numbers.com. Top 2019 Movies at the Worldwide Box Office, http://bit.ly/2019BOW
4 Considine, P. (2019, May 10). Spotlight on: Film trailers. IBC. http://bit.ly/FT4win
5 Olenski, S. (2018, August 15). 3 Reasons Why CMOs Should Embrace Experiential Marketing. Forbes.com, http://bit.ly/expCMO
6 Guttmann, A. (2021, January 15). Advertising Market Worldwide – statistics & facts. Statista. http://bit.ly/AdStatsWW
7 Crunchbase, Inc. (n.d.). Tool of North America – Crunchbase Company Profile & Funding. Crunchbase. Retrieved May 31, 2021, from https://www.crunchbase.com/organization/tool-of-north-america

8 Follows, S. (2018, November 21). How Long is the Average Movie Trailer? Stephen Follows. http://bit.ly/MTavg
9 StudioBinder. (2020, January 13). How to Make a Movie Trailer That Grabs Attention. http://bit.ly/MT-diy
10 Statista. (2021, February 11). Super Bowl TV Viewership in the U.S. 1990–2021. http://bit.ly/SBcount
11 Considine, P. (2019b, May 10). Spotlight on: Film Trailers. IBC. http://bit.ly/FT4win
12 Mediratta, S. (2016, September 27). World's Longest Music Video is of 24 Hours. Inshorts. http://bit.ly/24happ
13 James, G. (2019, August 13). Jeff Bezos, Mark Cuban, and Tony Robbins Don't PowerPoint. They Do This Instead. Inc.com. http://bit.ly/2KxuSGs
14 TED. (n.d.). The most popular TED Talks of all Time. TED Talks. Retrieved May 31, 2021, from http://bit.ly/talks25
15 Carnegie Mellon University. (n.d.). Randy Pausch's last Lecture. Retrieved May 31, 2021, from https://www.cmu.edu/randyslecture/
16 Andrews, A. (2018, April 18). Why Do We Need Presentation Skills? ZandaX. http://bit.ly/preso-y
17 Delgado, M. (2018, January 31). Small Business Websites in 2018 | Clutch.co. Clutch. http://bit.ly/Site_no
18 Maxwell, T. (2019, October 4). The Role of a Website Today. Forbes. http://bit.ly/Site2day
19 Maxwell, T. (2019a, March 15). The Essence of Social Media and Hospitality. Forbes. http://bit.ly/sm-party
20 mediakix. (2017, December 20). Instagram is Worth over $100 Billion [Chart]. http://bit.ly/ig_1b

Appendices

Topics Covered

Sample Cover and Campaign Planning Letter   169
Sample Proposal   171
Sample Letter Agreement   181
Sample Monthly Activity Report   184

Sample Cover and Campaign Planning Letter

From: Roger Darnell <rd@darnellworks.com>

Sent: Thursday, April 8, 2021 4:23 PM

To: Roger Darnell <rd@darnellworks.com>

Subject: Public relations proposal…

Hi Roger:

Thank you <u>very much</u> once again for inviting me to provide the attached proposal to address the public relations and marketing objectives we have discussed for yourself as an author and career guide.

Along with the proposal, you'll also find an agreement letter attached. These materials reflect an official start date of May 1, and I have entered a budget amount of $3,500 per month for a three-month campaign, which if all goes well, will then carry on a month-to-month basis.

Looking ahead, here are the steps I see as being important enough to consider putting them at the top of our agenda, subject to your feedback.

1. Revisit positioning and ensure it's as strong as possible for the foreseeable future
2. Clarify key business objectives to be served through PR campaign in the early going, and perhaps second-tier ones to be addressed down the road
3. Inventory the company's branding and its owned media channels, and discuss how those can be strengthened and used in unison to address our objectives
4. Inventory "news-worthy" developments and plan how and when to use those – with the goal of establishing a content calendar for use through year's end

5. Additional planning to support prioritized objectives – for example, media relations, business development, awards, speaking engagements, recruiting, etc.

<u>Homework to Gather Rocket Fuel for PR Launch</u>

1. List at least five media outlets you want to be sure we target through our efforts.
2. Please let me know if the company, or key individuals, is/are a member of any professional organization(s) – and share websites as applicable.
3. By mid-May, please be prepared to provide a summary for your online metaverse (social media channels, other online outposts) – identifying main contact(s) responsible for managing them. I expect this will include LinkedIn, Twitter, Instagram, Facebook, Vimeo, possibly YouTube etc., and even your website. I will expect to be part of the team weighing in on those channels, and can potentially be more "hands on." For those where you are wanting me to contribute, I'll be looking to be added to admins and/or given access in May (access not necessary for your website).
4. For discussions around Positioning

    i. Please provide five main keywords that you feel are the most important ideas/realms for us to focus on in our efforts, which to me, all fall under the heading of "marketing." Please also give me five secondary keywords.
    ii. Please review my PR proposal's section where I've provided competitors' boilerplates. Which is your favorite and least favorite, and why? Any other notes on anything you see there?
    iii. Please review and be prepared to discuss this article: http://bit.ly/Strong-Brand
    iv. Please review and be prepared to discuss this article: https://www.winwithoutpitching.com/ten-tests/

When reasonably possible, I do feel that spending some time together in person might be very helpful in our early going. If you agree, please advice on a date that might work for you. FYI, I would plan to cover my travel expenses but bill for time spent working together. Of course, we can also use Zoom to close the distance.

Very best wishes – Roger D., 1.828.424.7698

The Darnell Works Agency
https://www.darnellworks.com
https://linkedin.com/in/darnell

Sample Proposal

EXHIBIT A

ROGER DARNELL

Roger Darnell
Public Relations Proposal

Proposed Start of Campaign: May 1, 2021

ROGER DARNELL

THE DARNELL WORKS AGENCY
27 VALLE VISTA DRIVE
ASHEVILLE, NC 28804 USA
+1.828.424.7698 PHONE

**THE DARNELL WORKS AGENCY
STRATEGIC PUBLIC RELATIONS**

Roger Darnell
Public Relations Proposal   Page 1   4/8/21

Situation Analysis

Author, publisher, PR consultant, producer, and career guide Roger Darnell (RKD) is the principal of the Darnell Works Agency (DWA), the go-to PR firm for creative agencies, brands, and entertainment ventures. Since the agency's launch in 2000, DWA's clients have succeeded brilliantly, reflecting well on RKD's contributions. A widely published author and creator, RKD's career achievements leverage extensive qualifications in training and strategic marketing communications and span a wide array of high-profile business developments and productions. With the upcoming publication of two non-fiction books, the author is preparing to launch a new platform and support it with a savvy marketing campaign aimed at reaching all those interested in expanding their career opportunities in the communications and business – and helping to make career dreams come true. With an eye toward harnessing intelligent, proactive PR activities to attract and engage readers worldwide, the author is preparing to activate an intelligent PR and marketing campaign. From a promotional point of view, the forthcoming book one launch (expected in September) will provide a momentous storytelling opportunity. There are also many opportunities to use RKD's websites and social media presence to support the campaign, expand the author's strategic storytelling reach, and diligently, mindfully attract attention. Crafting sharp communications efforts to support new initiatives – and reaching out to the right audiences on timely bases with dedicated professional communications and media relations support – will compound new successes, while organically extending "presence of mind" among target audiences. A focused, sustained marketing campaign can also expand knowledge of the author's offerings, professionalism, capabilities, and expertise. Notably, DWA has a strong interest in the success of these efforts.

As an acknowledged expert in public and media relations with an exemplary track record for high-level success, and unique qualifications for serving your communications needs, I propose to partner with you to design and execute all PR-related aspects of your new strategic marketing plans … to professionally and creatively package and deliver inspired communications activities in support of your objectives, business developments, and dreams. With your groundbreaking work and evolving stories in the hands of a motivated, results-oriented, proven marketing communications professional, we will plan, launch, and maintain a proactive, integrated campaign effort that will propel your renown to new heights.

Approach

Over the past 30 years, I've handled marketing and publicity for scores of high-profile clients in advertising, branding, entertainment, media, film/TV production, design, software, Internet, and other high-tech industries, and I feel that my experience and capabilities are perfectly suited to leveraging the full power of PR in support of your objectives. A Scripps-Howard Fellowship-winning journalist and writer with professional credits spanning screenplays, television and video scripts, and scores of non-fiction articles in national and international magazines, I'm also an accomplished producer in new and traditional media. In addition to U.S. Air Force training in photojournalism, public affairs and instructional systems design, I have two Bachelor of Arts Communications degrees from the University of Central Florida, one in Film and a second in Radio/Television.

My successful record for converting business developments into solid media exposure will also greatly benefit you. I have many excellent and long-standing relationships with high-profile members of the media and analysts covering many industries, and my journalism background gives me the ability to engage and earn the respect of media professionals I'm contacting for the first – or the fiftieth – time. Also, based on my tenure at high-tech PR firm The Terpin Group in Los Angeles, my observations in networking with other top PR firms and the feedback I receive from working journalists, I know I'm on the leading edge when it comes to using today's most viable communications tools to pitch, package, and deliver stories and materials to the media – and also, directly to your targets.

Also worth noting in regard to the current economic climate, I know that the challenges currently faced by your audience members in all industries are increasing the difficulties associated with marketing at *any* level. Indeed, at this time, promoting a project typically demands the highest level of diligence, care and strategic consideration. Based upon my experiences in successfully navigating these waters, I approach every client promotional opportunity understanding that it may be best suited for a treatment ranging from "hands-off" to one allowing us to lead communications efforts across groups of major corporate executives and "rock stars" from all walks of life. Again, I always focus on finding the key tools, workflows, strategies, and **words** that can help us maximize efforts, and deftly using them to drive results in the right directions. To say the least, I will take great pride in doing my best work on your behalf.

Key Message

Successful PR programs begin with a strategically sound descriptive positioning statement. Ideally, each and every communication relates this key message, ensuring journalists and analysts understand what industry a company operates within, its marketplace stature, and its strategic perspective. This message is also a tool to help your partners and representatives maximize every networking opportunity. As we progress, I will expect ongoing collaboration to ensure the messaging used in our materials will be consistent and as effective as possible in addressing your prioritized objectives. For further consideration, here are some samples of positioning language I have gathered from your competitive landscape.

- **David C. Baker** is the author of five books, three of which focus on the central elements of the business of expertise: positioning, financial management, and leadership. David speaks regularly on more than 70 topics relevant to entrepreneurial expertise, from 20 executives to 5,000 live on TV, all over the world. He also regularly appears as a guest on ca. 15 different podcasts every month. David has worked with 900+ firms through the Total Business Review process. Engagements are remote or on-site, and each involves careful analysis and application to your specific situation. There are a half dozen options for working together. https://www.davidcbaker.com
- **Deirdre Breakenridge** is the CEO of Pure Performance Communications, a company that fuses strategic communications with innovative technology to impact business communications from consumer interest to brand loyalty and advocacy. Deirdre has been in PR and marketing for over 25 years, helping senior executives in mid-and-large organizations better communicate with their stakeholders. Deirdre also does reputation management and social media relations. She's a LinkedIn Learning

instructor and was an Adjunct Professor at NYU, and she has written many books including Answers for Modern Communicators, and her latest, Answers for Ethical Marketers. https://deirdrebreakenridge.com
- **Sarah Elkins** is a communications coach, keynote speaker, Strengths-Finders coach, author, and storyteller. Her work with Elkins Consulting guides teams to create environments that encourage and inspire authentic connections while improving connection at all levels. In addition, Sarah as the founder of the No Longer Virtual conference, a gathering of top LinkedIn personalities, to share knowledge and build in-person relationships. Forbes has called this conference one of the "six can't miss conferences in 2018." https://elkinsconsulting.com
- **Malcolm Gladwell** is the author of five New York Times bestsellers — The Tipping Point, Blink, Outliers, What the Dog Saw, and David and Goliath. He is also the co-founder of Pushkin Industries, an audio content company that produces the podcasts Revisionist History, which reconsiders things both overlooked and misunderstood, and Broken Record, where he, Rick Rubin, and Bruce Headlam interview musicians across a wide range of genres. Gladwell has been included in the TIME 100 Most Influential People list and touted as one of Foreign Policy's Top Global Thinkers. https://www.gladwellbooks.com
- **Tim Grahl** is the author of "Running Down a Dream" and "Your First 1000 Copies". For over a decade he has worked with top authors and creatives including Daniel H. Pink, Barbara Corcoran, Hugh MacLeod, Hugh Howey, Chip, and Dan Heath. He has run the campaigns to launch dozens of bestselling books and built and sold two companies. Through that time he also had a marriage that teetered towards divorce, suffered from anxiety attacks and a personality disorder, and had the IRS subpoena him. Tim hopes his story will inspire and help people during the pursuit of their dreams. https://www.runningdownadream.com
- **Joe Lazauskas** is Vice President at Contently, a media technology company that has helped over 100,000 creative freelancers get work and manage their careers. He is a regular contributor to Fast Company, and serves as Executive Editor of Contently's publications The Freelancer and The Content Strategist (winner of the 2016 Digiday Award for Best Brand Publication). Formerly a freelance media journalist, Joe has written for Forbes, AdWeek, and many other publications. His bestselling book, The Storytelling Edge, was published by Wiley in 2018. https://www.joelazer.com

- **Elise Mitchell**'s experience encompasses both entrepreneurial and corporate life. She is the founder of three companies – two in leadership development, one in public relations. Most notably, she is founder of Mitchell Communications Group, one of the top 10 fastest-growing public relations firms globally and a two-time Inc. 500/5000 fastest growing company. In 2013, Elise sold her firm to Dentsu, Inc., the world's largest ad agency, based in Tokyo. She led the successful integration of her firm over a five-year period in a newly established global parent company, Dentsu Aegis Network. Elise served as CEO of the Dentsu Aegis Public Relations Network, leading M&A efforts in public relations and collaborating with colleagues in nine countries to leverage growth opportunities and position the collective internationally. Today she advises clients through her own leadership and business consultancy. https://elisemitchell.com
- **Joanna Penn** writes non-fiction for authors and is an award-nominated, New York Times and USA Today bestselling thriller author as J.F. Penn. She's a podcaster and an award-winning creative entrepreneur. Her site, https://TheCreativePenn.com has been voted in the Top 100 sites for writers by Writer's Digest.
- **Dan Portnoy** is a writer/producer from the Boston Area, living in Los Angeles. He specializes in brand storytelling. His multi-media work focuses on combining beautiful metaphors with easy viewer comprehension. He works across branding, music videos, trailers, editorial, documentary, and advertising. He currently works through Portnoy Media Group. http://www.danportnoy.com
- **David Oakley** has been telling brand stories at BooneOakley for years. He has won many prestigious honors, including the Kaopectate Award in the eighth grade for having diarrhea of the mouth. His first book, Why Is Your Name Upside Down?, is full of stories from his life in advertising. Despite this, he was recently inducted into the North Carolina Advertising Hall of Fame. He lives with his wife Claire and their dog Walter in Charlotte, where they raised Sydney and Lucas. He loves his family very much and hopes they still love him after reading Nobody Eats Parsley. http://www.davidoakley.com
- **Vern Oakley** is a television and film director based in New Jersey. He is also the founder of Tribe Pictures. Oakley received top honors at the International Film and Television Festival for his direction of the

Emmy Award-winning children's television series Reading Rainbow. His work as an editor on the documentary The Chemical People for PBS garnered him an Emmy nomination. His first theatrical release feature, A Modern Affair, starring Stanley Tucci and Lisa Eichhorn, was invited to multiple festivals. It showed on HBO and was distributed by Columbia TriStar, which he produced and directed. His feature Paraty, a USA-Brazil co-production is in the preproduction stage. https://vernoakley.com

Strategic Objectives

PR goals for this campaign will include proactively driving targeted editorial and news coverage to deliver solid returns on all of your campaign investments. To accomplish this, I propose the following objectives:

- Continuously review and consider refining the positioning language and communications toolset for your business, building upon your unique value propositions, to always present strengths, capabilities, and service offerings as strategically as possible.
- Prove to key audiences that your expertise, services, principals, key personnel, clients, and original projects are extraordinary.
- Demonstrate the viability of your vision(s) and business model(s) by promoting your abilities to creatively fulfill important needs for your clients.
- Package principals', key personnel's, and key clients' practical beliefs and ideologies into press releases, testimonials, case studies, and other strategic communications pieces.
- Identify and pursue the most strategically valuable editorial opportunities.
- Track, evaluate, and capitalize on opportunities to increase your credibility and stature by supporting and (whenever possible) publicizing high-profile business developments and any awards related to partners, personnel, or client works.
- Package interesting ideas as byline articles, announcements, speaking topic proposals, and/or publications related to your unique perspectives, beliefs, and ideologies.
- Strategically plan for any risks or contingencies that might affect your image or objectives.

Roger Darnell
Public Relations Proposal   Page 7   4/8/21

Target Media

Past editorial exposure I've received for my clients includes coverage in all forms of mainstream and trade media, as prescribed by client objectives and developments. I'll use our agreed-upon messages and strategies to influence the widest possible range of audiences of importance to you. My comprehensive database will be expanded, updated, and fine-tuned as needed to support your specific promotional objectives.

Ongoing Monthly Services

The following services are available and will be provided as prescribed according to your priorities and budget in a given month.

- **Market Positioning.** Evaluate current strategy and core capabilities in terms of managing, extending, or expanding client relationships. Focus in on overall position, image, and market strategies to maximize strategic opportunities.
- **Corporate Image-Building Campaign.** Generate positive buzz in circles of various influencers via strategic mentions of your developments in high-profile industry round-ups and trend stories, and by helping to build, manage and/or execute a sophisticated social media campaign.
- **News Bureau.** Generate news releases to promote new developments, strengthen client/vendor alliances, and provide a flow of strategic information about your developments and major activities to key media outlets. Develop/refine media kits, including company backgrounders, bios, press releases, and media alerts.
- **One-on-One Interviews.** Introduce principals to influential media to explain company mission and/or latest business or project developments.
- **Awards Competitions.** Identify, monitor, and facilitate submissions for awards competitions of value to RKD, as prescribed.
- **Speaking Engagements.** Identify and facilitate speaking opportunities at influential trade shows and conferences to complement other image-building elements of the campaign, as advised.
- **Networking and BizDev Opportunity Research and Development.** Mine RKD's marketplaces of interest, sharing ideas and pursuing them, as requested.

Project Costs[1]

These details and others I'm suggesting for our partnership are summarized in the accompanying letter agreement. Based upon my past experience, I make every effort to present terms that offer us both the fairest working arrangement possible, including the commitment to monitoring the level of service I'm providing you and to consider making any adjustments necessary to meet your bottom-line objectives.

Monthly Retainer of U.S. $3,500: This suggested basic retainer, payable before the commencement of work at the beginning of each month, is an estimate of actual hours expected to be billed for the basic campaign, according to a standard hourly rate of U.S. $215 per hour.[2]

Expenses: Although every effort will be made to minimize expenses, typical expenses can include postage, photocopying, telephone, mileage, parking, delivery services, clipping services, and press release distribution services. Out-of-town travel expenses include airfare, hotel, transportation, parking and meals. If approved monthly expenses total less than U.S. $75, they will not be charged. There is no mark-up on expenses.

Availability

This proposal is targeted toward a launch date of May 1, 2021. My sincere enthusiasm for your business and imperatives, along with my solid writing capabilities, experience and contacts, will allow us to ignite a powerful start of the campaign right away. I can currently affirm my availability to serve you during this period according to these specifications – and your prompt response to this proposal will put us in business together.

Summary

I consider joining your team and serving your communications needs to be a great honor and an exciting privilege; I truly believe that by joining our capabilities, we will succeed in delivering an extraordinary return on a solid investment into a dynamic PR campaign. I encourage you to review my profile on LinkedIn, and to let me know if I can provide further information to help you assess my terms, professional qualifications, reputation, and/or capabilities. I also look forward to hearing your feedback on this proposal at your

Roger Darnell
Public Relations Proposal   Page 9   4/8/21

earliest convenience, and to partnering with you to launch your campaign according to your specifications ASAP.

Sincerely,

Roger Darnell

Notes

1. Terms detailed in attached letter agreement.
2. This is $5 above the going rate in 2000 for a VP/GM at the LA-based high-tech PR firm where I worked at that time.

Sample Letter Agreement

Thursday, April 8, 2021

Roger Darnell
Asheville, NC 28804

Dear Roger:

This document will serve as an Engagement Letter (the "Agreement") between The Darnell Works Agency (the "Agency") and Roger Darnell (the "Client"), the "parties." As agreed, Agency will perform select marketing services as described in the attached proposal (Exhibit A). The initial term shall commence on **May 1, 2021** (the "Commencement Date") for three calendar months, ending **July 31, 2021** (the "Term"). Upon completion of the Term, this Agreement, and rights and obligations of the parties, will continue to be in force and effect on a month-to-month basis until termination of this Agreement as provided herein below.

Client promises to pay Agency a retainer in the amount of U.S. $3,500.00 per month for basic and optional services, as described in Exhibit A. The monthly retainer will be applied to the Agency's statements for client-directed services rendered on an hourly basis. In the event, the hourly wages total less than the retainer amount in a given period, the unused portion of that period's retainer shall be carried over into the following period. Agency's hourly fee is U.S. $215.00 per hour. Any work performed beyond the monthly retainer will require Client's previous consent. Client agrees to pay the first month's retainer of U.S. $3,500.00 upon execution of this

Engagement Letter. During the first month of services, the Client will be billed a second retainer amount of U.S. $3,500.00 for services to be rendered during the second month that this Agreement is in effect. Payment of the second retainer billing, and the billing for all months thereafter, is due no later than ten (10) days after the Due Date.

From time to time after end of the Term of the Agreement, Client and Agency shall use reasonable efforts to review the appropriate level of services being provided by Agency to Client, and to consider making an appropriate adjustment in the monthly retainer for succeeding calendar months. If either party reasonably believes a material discrepancy exists between the amount of the monthly retainer and the level of Agency's services and the expected future services, the parties may renegotiate in good faith the monthly retainer and other terms and conditions of this Agreement. Any modification, amendment, waiver or assignment of this Agreement must be by mutual consent in writing.

Failure to pay any monthly retainer and/or for any billed service items no later than ten (10) days of the Due Date is a breach of the terms of this Engagement Letter and may result in suspension of Agency activities.

Either party may terminate this Agreement with or without cause at any time after completion of the first month of the Term, by giving no less than ten (10) days written notice prior to termination. Client acknowledges that the Agency has allocated substantial time to Client's services and that Agency has spent and will spend substantial uncompensated time in preparing to perform and in performing Agency's obligations as set forth in this Engagement Letter. In the event that Client has given proper notice of termination of services, or otherwise suspends or limits Agency's services prior to the end of the monthly term, Client agrees that Client will pay Agency for services for the entire ten-day termination period.

This Agreement shall be binding on and shall inure to the benefit of and be enforceable by the parties hereto and their respective legal representatives. Nothing contained in this Agreement shall be deemed to benefit, directly or indirectly, any person or entity other than the parties hereto.

Any dispute under or relating to the terms of this Agreement, or the breach, validity or legality thereof, shall be submitted to binding arbitration in accordance with the rules promulgated by the American Arbitration Association, and any arbitration award may be entered in any court having jurisdiction thereof. The prevailing party shall be entitled to recover any and all reasonable outside attorneys' fees and other costs incurred in the enforcement of the terms of this Agreement or for the breach hereof. This arbitration provision shall remain in full force and effect notwithstanding the nature of any claim or defense hereunder.

This Agreement contemplates the Agency's and the Client's (the "parties") entire agreement, and supersedes any and all prior or contemporaneous agreements, whether written or oral.

Each of the parties hereto has been advised to consult its respective legal representatives prior to entering into this Agreement. Furthermore, each of the parties acknowledges that it has participated in the negotiation and completion of this Agreement. This Agreement shall be governed and interpreted in accordance with the laws of the State of North Carolina.

I am delighted to be chosen as your public relations representative, and I look forward to an extremely rewarding partnership.

Sincerely,

Roger Darnell

By my signature below, I represent that I have been authorized to bind the Client to this agreement. I further represent that the corporation is in good standing under the laws of the State of _____.

Accepted:

By: _____
     Roger Darnell

Date: _____

Sample Monthly Activity Report

```
Date 10/29/12        The Darnell Works Agency
Time 12:00pm         Client Billing Worksheet
=======================Selection Criteria=======================
Date range:          10/1/12 through 10/28/12 (COMPLETE REPORT
                     FOR PERIOD)
Client:              ATTIK
================================================================
Address:             ATTIK, A Division of Dentsu America
                     85 Second Street, 6th Floor
                     San Francisco. CA. 94105
Phone 1:             415-284-2600
In reference to:     PR Campaign
================================================================
    Date/Slip#       HOURS

[SCION = 16.09]

   10/1/2012         0.33
#11796   SCION: Had some corresp. w/ RP about handling on
account based on request from Scion PR contact CT; checked out
a few stories that popped up in the media based on Pixo's
outreach, had a bit more f/u w/ PR contacts there.

   10/2/2012         0.62
#11804   SCION: Did some more media tracking and shared some
of the latest pickups on s/m channels; reached out to Simon
and had brief chat to discuss Scion 'response' to Ad Age
article; emailed CT @ Scion to let him know I'll be back
in-touch ASAP i/r/t C8 campaign writing 'next steps'; had some
corresp. w/ RP about Scion handling, also had a chat to
discuss it and sorted strategy.

                                                    -continued-
```

Date 10/29/12   The Darnell Works Agency
Time 12:00pm   Client Billing Worksheet   Page 2
==

   Date/Slip#   HOURS

   10/4/2012   1.13
   #11815 SCION: Reviewed all the materials I could get my
   hands on for C8, started gathering some notes, wrote to MO to
   request more info ASAP and called CT to discuss next steps;
   did some planning for upcoming initiatives.

   10/5/2012   1.76
   #11822 SCION: Tracked media exposure, contacted WELOVEAD
   to touch-base on WMY submission; had a chat w/ CT to discuss
   PR for Motivate, including some promotional ideas - afterward,
   shared notes, media contact at Thrillist, notes on Digital LA
   events, etc.; also updated RP; also wrote to ATTIK account
   team to share idea for trying to shape-up editorial based on
   Motivate campaign media buys; tracked media exposure, posted
   TSFE item to ATTIK's FB.

   10/8/2012   2.14
   #11826 SCION: Did more research and work on writing-up C8/
   Motivate story - sent second pass to CT w/ notes.

   10/9/2012   0.32
   #11834 SCION: Had more corresp. w/ CT to set plans to chat
   about Motivate on Thursday; spent a little time to review
   objectives and gather ideas for upcoming pushes for Motivate
   campaign for agency.

   10/11/2012   0.22
   #11844 SCION: Called CT to discuss Motivate, LM - explored
   more of new WMY campaign landing page on Scion.com to check
   out backstories, videos, etc.

   10/15/2012   0.05
   #11848 SCION: Still awaiting word from CT @ Scion on
   Motivate campaign - updated agenda.

   10/16/2012   0.50
   #11854 SCION: Gathered notes ahead of today's call w/ Craig -
   had call, made plans to follow-up next week - everything is still
   aiming toward 10/25 for "Motivate" announcements.

                                                    -continued-

Date 10/29/12   The Darnell Works Agency
Time 12:00pm   Client Billing Worksheet   Page 3
==
   Date/Slip#   HOURS

   10/17/2012   0.23
   #11865 SCION: Wrote to account team again to request input
   for Motivate story and gave them an update on timing/info flow
   from Scion; also reached out to CT again to request any
   updates ASAP.

   10/18/2012   0.13
   #11869 SCION: Looked at brief notes provided by account
   team, updated schedule for next-steps based on latest
   exchanges w/ CT @ Scion.

   10/24/2012   3.58
   #11890 SCION: Reviewed Scion's Motivate release and
   provided some feedback to CT @ Scion; organized materials and
   info provided by account team, drafted news release, sent it
   to execs w/ notes; had chats w/ SN and RP to discuss Motivate
   release and PR campaign ideas; updated ATTIK's Motivate
   release, sent it to CT at Scion w/ notes.

   10/25/2012   4.40
   #11894 SCION: Gathered notes for moving forward on Motivate
   campaign push - reviewed assets, sent notes to Darren about
   print ad, also went to Scion.com/motivate and generated
   screengrabs to ensure what I have is the final/approved
   artwork; found Motivate artwork on Scion's FB page, shared it
   on ATTIK's FB page w/ link into program section; reviewed
   release, realized I need to add info about illustrated
   elements - updated, sent note to RP to run revision past him
   and inquire about mention of Darren - also reached out to
   RP by phone and left VM; had chat w/ RP, sorted 'issue' of
   illustrator mention w/ SZ and RL, then finalized materials,
   authored and posted EPK site content, authored and tested
   pitch, then distributed story to targeted media outlets,
   including submitting it into SHOOT's Publicity Wire and PRN for
   distribution at 2pm PDT; had a bit of media f/u w/ editor from
   BrandChannel - sent link to BrandChannel story to CT w/ notes.

   10/26/2012   0.68
   #11901 SCION: Tracked media exposure, sent PRN
   ReleaseWatch report & more clips to execs; had f/u w/ KG @
   MediaPost, set/coordinated phoner w/ RL.

   [GENERAL = 5.59]

                                                          -continued-

Appendices   187

```
Date 10/29/12        The Darnell Works Agency
Time 12:00pm         Client Billing Worksheet                Page 4
================================================================
   Date/Slip#        HOURS
```

10/1/2012   0.21
#11795 GENERAL: Had some corresp. w/ RP to fill him in on my contacts Tracy Chandler and Andre Stringer and "connect the dots" between them (now based in LA) and Under Armour, per my discussion last week with Dave H.

10/2/2012   0.25
#11805 GENERAL: Had some corresp. w/ RP about introducing ex-Shilo talents (now based in LA) to him directly, also had a chat to discuss it and sorted strategy for next steps; sent query from student to GC w/ interview request.

10/3/2012   0.38
#11811 GENERAL: Had some f/u corresp. on latest media outreach; reviewed and updated PR agenda and sent it to execs w/ notes; more corresp. w/ GC on student interview request; had corresp. w/ contact from SFBT on survey for annual ad agency listing.

10/4/2012   0.61
#11816 GENERAL: Reached back to RP and TC to "re-introduce" them and set up get-together; had biweekly chat w/ DH, discussed his sales tools and ATTIK's boilerplate; did some planning for upcoming initiatives.

10/8/2012   0.12
#11827 GENERAL: Had corresp. w/ RP about SFBT Ad Agency list, survey, etc.; also sent over call for entries from EFFIE Awards.

10/9/2012   0.20
#11829 GENERAL: Added some new media targets to short-list for media outreach on upcoming projects.

10/11/2012   1.37
#11840 GENERAL: Had corresp. and phone call w/ Publicity Wire editor at SHOOT on discussion of embedding reels in news releases; tracked media exposure, updated ITN listing on EPK site, sent link and clippings to execs w/ notes; sent execs (including OP and CT at Scion) heads-up on upcoming issue of CommArts hitting the streets on 10/29.

-continued-

Appendices

```
Date 10/29/12        The Darnell Works Agency
Time 12:00pm         Client Billing Worksheet                    Page 5
================================================================
   Date/Slip#        HOURS
```

10/16/2012   0.10
#11856 GENERAL: Brief corresp. w/ RP about RN resignation - also sent him note with "PR paper trail" on Bacardi.

10/17/2012   0.30
#11866 GENERAL: Updated PR agenda and sent it to execs w/ notes - had a bit of f/u corresp. w/ MK, "Kraft" now off our agenda.

10/18/2012   0.72
#11870 GENERAL: Had some corresp. w/ DH about next chat, aiming for 11/1 ~ also responded to his notes about some sales copy he's working on; did some research on 'agency of the year' competitions, calls for entry, submission deadlines, etc.

10/22/2012   1.33
#11882 GENERAL: Did some more research, added more contact information and details for potential editorial targets for upcoming project stories.

[MONDELEZ = 0.23]

10/3/2012   0.23
#11813 MONDELEZ: Did some research, tracked-down today's releases from Mondelez and sent links to execs w/ notes.

[MSOG = 0.05]

10/15/2012   0.05
#11853 MSOG: Sent link/note to execs about "Goodworks Effie" call for entries.

```
--------------------------------------------------------------------
TOTAL BILLABLE TIME CHARGES                    21.96     $3,624.32
====================================================================
TOTAL NEW CHARGES                                        $3,624.32
RETAINER FOR PERIOD                                     -3,000.00
====================================================================
NEW BALANCE                                                $624.32
| DISCOUNT                                                -624.32 |
====================================================================
TOTAL NEW BALANCE                                            $0.00
```

*** THANK YOU FOR THE OPPORTUNITY TO SERVE YOU. ***

Index

Note: *Italicized* and **bold** page numbers refer to figures and tables.

ABJ *see* Austin Business Journal (ABJ)
academic programs 116
action plans 142–151; focus 149; Objectives and Key Results 143–145, *144*; strategic plans of action 145–148
Activia Training 160
Activity Report 26, 27
Adobe After Effects 158
Adobe Illustrator 158
Adobe Premiere 158
AdRants.com 110
advanced PR account management 49–71; content marketing 63–66; distribution 56–58; external events 67–69; integrated news bureau 49–52; internal events 66–67; interviews 61–62; media coverage 62–63; media relations for external events 69–70; news, strategic making of 52–54, 53; news release development 56–58; non-paid editorial exclusive 58–59; pitching 56–58; preparing to pitch 55–56; search engine optimization 63; social media 63–66, *64*; strategy 56–58; wide news release distribution 59–61
advanced tactics 80–86
advertising 84–85, 155–157
Advertising Value Equivalency (AVE) 50, 51
agency business 3–4
agency management 91–107; arena 92–95; branding 97–98; business brands 97–98; business development 98–100; cash flow 103–104; customer service 100–101; integrated marketing 101–103; Investor Relations 104–105; investors 104–105; leadership 95–95; objectives 96–97; project flow 103–104; reporting 105–106
AgencySpotter.com 102
AICP *see* Association of Independent Commercial Producers (AICP)
AICP Show 115
AIGA *see* American Institute of Graphic Arts (AIGA)
Air Force Reserve Officer Training Corps 6
Alpha 35–37, 74, 75, 104, 113, 134
AMA *see* American Marketing Association (AMA)
Amazon 43, 66
AMC: "Pitch, The" 84–85
AMEC *see* International Association for Measurement and Evaluation of Communication (AMEC)
American Institute of Graphic Arts (AIGA) 114
American Marketing Association (AMA) 114
American Press Institute 64
American Speech-Language-Hearing Association (ASHA) 61–62
AMH *see* Asheville Music Hall (AMH)
analyst and influencer relations 82
"Anatomy of a Marketing Plan" (VanAuken) 136
Andreessen Horowitz 44

Index

Andrews, Ashley: "Why Do We Need Presentation Skills" 160
Apple 158; Worldwide Developers Conference 161
Approach 18, 19, 173–174
arena 92–95
art and craft of presentation 152–165; advertising 155–157; commercials 155–157; digital and physical savant 163–164; music videos 157–159; presentations 154–155; sales presentations 160–161; social networks 162–163; stage presentations 159–160; trailers 157–159; websites 161–162
ASHA see American Speech-Language-Hearing Association (ASHA)
Asheville Music Hall (AMH) 104, 105
Association of Computing Machinery 114
Association of Independent Commercial Producers (AICP) 114
ATTIK 84, 91, 102, 103, 105, 124–126, 129, 133
Audiovisual and Integrated Experience Association, The (AVIXA) 114
Austin Business Journal (ABJ) 42
Avenue M 104–105
AVE see Advertising Value Equivalency (AVE)
Avid Media Composer 158
AVIXA see Audiovisual and Integrated Experience Association, The (AVIXA)
award shows 85–86

Bacon's Information 112
Baer, Jay 65; "Youtility" 63, 161
Baker, David C. 31–33, 44, 126–128, 174; "Business of Expertise, The" 31, 32
Baker, Randy 114
Balanced Scorecard 137, 149
Barcelona Principles 51
BEACH PRO system 62
Beane, Molly (Borchers) 50, 52
big deal 43–44
Billing 27–28
bios 55–56
Bizzabo 67–69
Boggs, Lacy 139
Bonniol, Bob 33
branding 97–98

Breakenridge, Deirdre 70, 174–175
Brooks' Law 86
Buckingham, Marcus: "Now, Discover Your Strengths" 121
business brands 97–98
business development 98–100
"Business of Expertise, The" (Baker) 31, 32
Business Wire 60
BusinessWire 112–113

Cameron, Glen: "Public Relations Strategies and Tactics" 44–45
campaign planning letter 169–170
Carmichael, Evan 41
CASE Currents Magazine 51
cash flow 103–104
CFO see Chief Financial Officer (CFO)
C4D see Maxon Cinema 4D (C4D)
CGI see Computer-Generated Imagery (CGI)
Chamber of Commerce 114
Chartered Institute of Public Relations, The 114
Chief Financial Officer (CFO) 44
Chief Marketing Officer 100
Clark, Doreen 50, 52
Client Activity Organizer **148**
Client Journal 146, 151
client presentations 83
Clifton, Donald O.: "Now, Discover Your Strengths" 121
CliftonStrengths assessment 121
CLIO Awards 115
CNN 46
CODE see Content, Organization, Delivery and Effect (CODE)
Collins, Jim: "Good to Great: Why Some Companies Make the Leap ... And Others Don't" 74
commercials 155–157
Communications Consultant's Foundation 11, 134, 161
communications planning fire drill 24–25
company backgrounder 55
Computer-Generated Imagery (CGI) 158
Content, Organization, Delivery and Effect (CODE) 83
content marketing 63–66, 81
Copy Platform 164
Corcoran, Barbara 175

Index

Crawford, Ilse 122–123
Crest National 153, 159
crowdfunders 42
Customer Experience (CX) 66, 76, 81, 126
customer service 100–101
CX see Customer Experience (CX)

Darnell, Beth 119
Darnell, Roger 34
Darnell's Law 124, 149
Darnell Works Agency, The (DWA) 1, 7, 17, 18, 20, 24, 26, 32, 41–42, 68, 91, 98–101, 109, 114, 115, 119, 120, 122, 127, 153, 172
"Day We Closed the News Bureau, The" (Simpson) 51
Deeb, George 43
Dentsu 124
digital and physical savant 163–164
diligence-driven demand, finding 109–111
direct marketing 84–85
DiSC Profile 121
distribution 56–58
Dow Chemical 45–46
drive for superiority 34
DVI Group 64, 65
DWA see Darnell Works Agency, The (DWA)
Dynamic Relationship 18

Effie Awards 85
Electronic Press Kit (EPK) 56, 62
elevator pitch 33–34
"Elevator Pitch" (Entrepreneur Magazine) 56
Elkins, Sarah 175
Elliott, Stuart 58
engagement 20–22
Enns, Blair 19, 31–32, 34, 44, 102, 126
Entrepreneur Magazine 34, 56, 134, 136, 137
EPK see Electronic Press Kit (EPK)
Etchison, Richard 58–59
Exit strategies and tactics 126–128
external communications spectrum 36–37, **37**
external events 67–69; media relations for 69–70
extracurricular activities 116

Facebook 43, 63, 110, 163, 164
Fast Company 41, 43
fear of missing out (FOMO) 68, 79

financial objectives 42–43
Flush Strategy 78–79, 82, 84, 86, 113; strong suits for **79**
focus 149
Follows, Stephen 157
FOMO see fear of missing out (FOMO)
Forbes 40, 53, 64, 125
Forbes Agency Council 162
formal communications planning 24
Forrester Research 139
From Molly with Love 50

Gallop, Cindy 117
Garfinkel, G.M. Mike 120
"Getting Started in Consulting" (Weiss) 25
GEVME 66, 67
Gilbert, Daniel 122
Giles, Sunnie 86
Gladwell, Malcolm 174–175
Glossy, Inc. 98
GoFundMe 42, 47
Goodson, Scott 98
"Good to Great: Why Some Companies Make the Leap ... And Others Don't" (Collins) 74
Goodwill Industries International 65
Google 43, 66
Grahl, Tim 175
Greenberg, Karl: "Noise Five" 124, 126
Greene, Robert 142, 147
Greiner Curve 35, 36, 126

Halbur, Alex 126–127
Hall, Steve 110
Harbridge, Lori-Ann 106
Harry 79
HBO 7, 74
Headlam, Bruce 175
headshots 56
Heath, Chip 175
Heath, Dan 175
Higgins, Ronnie 67
High-Quality (HQ) strategy 75–77, 76, 81–82, 84, 86; strong suits for **77**
Hootsuite 163
Hoovers.com 112
Hope, Bob 81
Hoque, Faisal 41, 43
Howey, Hugh 175

"How to Make a Movie Trailer that Grabs Attention" 157
HQ see High-Quality (HQ) strategy
Huffington Post 50, 53

Ikea 43
Indiegogo 42, 47
industry gatherings 115
Initial Public Offering (IPO) 44, 45
Instagram 63, 110, 163, 164
integrated marketing 101–103
integrated news bureau 49–52
internal communications spectrum 35–36, 35, **36**
internal events 66–67
International Association for Measurement and Evaluation of Communication (AMEC) 51, 52
International Public Relations Association, The 114
International Television Association (ITVA) 114, 115
interviews 61–62, 81–82
"inverted pyramid" approach 55–56, 55
InvestorPlace.com 44
Investor Relations (IR) 39, 44–46, 104–105; foundations of 46–47
Investor Relations Charter™ (IRC) Competency Framework 46–47; Code of Conduct 47
investors 41–42; pitch 41; seeking 39–41
IPO see Initial Public Offering (IPO)
IR see Investor Relations (IR)
ITA Group 66
ITVA see International Television Association (ITVA)

Jackson, Michael 158
James, Geoffrey 159
Joiner, Erich 156
Jordan, Jeff 44
J.R. O'Dwyer Company 92

Kaplan, R. S. 137, 138
key message 174–177
Key Performance Indicator 2
kick-off 22–23
Kickstarter 42, 47

Kim, Jen 122
King, Martin Luther, Junior 159
Knowles, Brett 137–139, 143
Kohnstamm, Josh 122
Kohnstamm Communications 122, 123

"Last Lecture, The" (Zaslow) 160
Lawson-Zilai, Lauren 65
Lazauskas, Joe 175
leadership, and management 95–96
"Leading Through the Turn" (Mitchell) 121, 123
Lee, Stan 161
Lego Group 43, 65
"lemonade stand" approach 36
letter agreement 20–22
Letter of Assignment 69
Leviathan 92
LinkedIn 63, 110, 163
Lopes, Matthew 65

MacLeod, Hugh 175
MAP see Marketing Action Plan (MAP)
Marketing Action Plan (MAP) 145, 147–149, 151
MarSciTechTainment 110
Maslow, Abraham 122
"Mastery" (Greene) 142
Maverick Strategy 79–80, 84, 86; strong suits for **80**
Maxon Cinema 4D (C4D) 158
Maxwell, T.: "Role of a Website Today, The" 162
McLuhan, Marshall: *Medium is the Massage, The* 152
McNeill, Don 14–15
McNeill PR Triangle, The 14–15, 104
media: alert 56; coverage 62–63; kit 56; relations 81; relations for external events 69–70; researching 111–114
Mediakix 164
Medium 110, 164
Medium is the Massage, The (McLuhan) 152
Meetup.com 114
Mills, General: Box Tops for Education program 16
Mission.org 64

Index

Mitchell, Elise 95, 123–124, 126, 128, 176; "Leading Through the Turn" 121, 123
Mitchell Communications 97, 105
MODE Studios 33
Muck Rack 113
music videos 157–159
"Myth: PR Campaigns Can't Be Measured" (Clark) 50

NAB *see* National Association of Broadcasters, The (NAB)
NASA 100; Mars Exploration Program 78
National Association of Broadcasters, The (NAB) 114
National Investor Relations Institute (NIRI) 46, 117; Code of Ethics 47; "Fundamentals of Investor Relations and Service Provider Showcase" 47
Needham, Simon 124
Needs Analysis 13, 14, 93, 135, 146
Netflix 66
news, strategic making of 52–54, 52
news release 55; development 56–58
New York Times, The 2, 58, 111; T Brand Studio 81
Next Web, The 42
Nickelodeon Studios 114
Nike 157
NIRI *see* National Investor Relations Institute (NIRI)
"Noise Five" (Greenberg) 124, 126
non-paid editorial exclusive 58–59
Norton, D. P. 137, 138
"Now, Discover Your Strengths" (Clifton and Buckingham) 121

Oakley, David 176
Oakley, Vern 176–177
Obama, Barack 110
objectives 96–97
Objectives and Key Results (OKRs) 143–145, *144*, 149
O'Brien, Mark 63, 66
Ochman, B.L. 112
O'Dwyer Company 1, 92
Office of Communications and Marketing 52
OKRs *see* Objectives and Key Results (OKRs)

Olivier, Clay 42, 43
Ongoing Monthly Services 20, 178–179
Orchard Point Group 121
original events 82

P&G *see* Procter & Gamble (P&G)
Patel, Neil 64
Pausch, Randy 160
Penn, Joanna 176
Pink, Daniel H. 175
Pinterest 63, 110, 164
"Pitch, The" (AMC) 84–85
pitch(ing) 56–58, 61; elevator 33–34; investor 41; preparing to 55–56
Portnoy, Dan 176
positioning 30–34
POSTAR model 75, 96
PostWorks New York 24, 136
PR *see* Public Relations (PR)
PR accounts, winning and managing 11–29; billing 27–28; communications planning fire drill 24–25; engagement 20–22; formal communications planning 24; initial interview 12–17; kick-off 22–23; letter agreement 20–22; proposal 17–20; record-keeping 25–27; time 25–27
presentations 154–155
press kit 56
press release 55
Prince's Trust, The 91
Pritchard, Marc 73
PR Newswire (PRN, now Cision) 60, 65, 112–113; Cision Communications Cloud 113
Procter & Gamble (P&G) 73–74, 85, 104
professional development 108–118; diligence-driven demand, finding 109–111; further resources 116–117; industry gatherings 115–116; media, researching 111–114; trade associations 114–115
professional education 116
Professional Writing 18, 19
project costs 179
project flow 103–104
Project Management Triangle 74–75
Promax 114
PromaxBDA Annual Conferences 115

Index

promo items 84
promotions 84
proposal 17–20
Prosper Group 126, 128
PRSA *see* Public Relations Society of America (PRSA)
PRWeb.com 60
Public Relations (PR) 1, 108, 109, 134; accounts, winning and managing *see* PR accounts, winning and managing; advanced account management 49–71; agency business 3–4; agenda 146; client services 2–3; master toolset 4
Public Relations Consultants Association, The 114
Public Relations Society of America (PRSA) 114, 123
"Public Relations Strategies and Tactics" (Wilcox and Cameron) 44–45
public speaking 83

QuickBooks 26
Quora.com 54

rainmakers 98
Rampton, J. 135
Ravikant, Naval 95
Raz, Karen 119–120
record-keeping 25–27
ReCourses, Inc. 127
Recourses New Business Summit (2012) 122
REI: #OptOutside policy 16
reporting 105–106
Request for Proposal (RFP) 155
Return on Investment (ROI) 49, 52, 56, 62, 63, 66, 67, 74, 100, 101, 103, 117, 134, 145
RFP *see* Request for Proposal (RFP)
right marketing plan 133–140
ROI *see* Return on Investment (ROI)
"Role of a Website Today, The" (Maxwell) 162
Rowling, J.K. 159
Rubin, Rick 175

sales presentations 160–161
Sample, Kim 127
sample cover 169–170
sample letter agreement 181–183
sample monthly activity report 184–188
sample proposal 171–180
Samsung 43
Sarofsky, Erin 91
SBTDC *see* Small Business and Technology Development Center (SBTDC)
scaling 119–123; strategies 123–126; tactics 123–126
Schwab, Michelle 121
search engine optimization (SEO) 63, 103
SEC *see* Securities and Exchange Commission (SEC)
Securities and Exchange Commission (SEC) 44, 45
SEGD *see* Society for Experiential Graphic Design, The (SEGD)
SEO *see* search engine optimization (SEO)
shares of communications 150
Shaw, G. Scott 32, 97, 98
SIGGRAPH *see* Special Interest Group on Computer Graphics and Interactive Techniques (SIGGRAPH)
Simply Framed 62
Simpson, Christopher 51, 52
SimpsonScarboroug 51
Situation Analysis 13, 18, 19, 172–173
Small Business and Technology Development Center (SBTDC) 136
Snapchat 63, 163, 164
social media 63–66, 64
social media release 55
social networks 162–163
Society for Experiential Graphic Design, The (SEGD) 114
Society of Digital Agencies, The (SoDA) 114
SoDA *see* Society of Digital Agencies, The (SoDA)
Solaris, Julius 68
Sommerville, James 124, 125
sounding out the right strategy 74–75
Southwest Airlines 139
Spark Factory, The 153
Special Interest Group on Computer Graphics and Interactive Techniques (SIGGRAPH) 114

Spotify 158
stage presentations 159–160
Statista 158
Steady Strategy 76–77, 83, 84, 86, 113; strong suits for **78**
Stephaniuk, Shannon 98
Stewart, Joan 56, 57
Stitch Fix 78
"Storytelling Edge, The" 83
Strategic Marketing Plan 24
Strategic Objectives 20, 138, 177–178
strategic plans of action 145–148
strategy 56–58
Strategy Maps 137–139, *138*, 149
StrawberryFrog 98
StudioBinder 157
Sudmann, Lars 83, 160
SWOT (Strengths, Weaknesses, Opportunities, and Threats) 99
SXSW 69

Target Media 20, 178
Taulli, Tom 44
TEA *see* Themed Entertainment Association, The (TEA)
TechNewsWorld 69
TED Talk 5, 122, 154, 159, 160, 165
Terpin, Michael 17
Themed Entertainment Association, The (TEA) 114
The Terpin Group (TTG) 7, 11, 17–21, 25–27, 30, 50–51, 60, 78, 101, 106, 112, 119, 120, 142, 153, 173
TikTok 63, 164
Time 25–27
Toyota: Scion 125, 126
trade associations 114–115
trade shows 85
trailers 157–159
Travis, Will 125
TTG *see* The Terpin Group (TTG)
Tumblr 110, 164
12manage.com 137–138
Twitch 164
Twitter 63, 110, 111, 117, 118, 163, 164

UCF *see* University of Central Florida (UCF)
Ultimate Events 68
Universal Studios 49
University of Central Florida (UCF) 6; Cinematography Association 115
U.S. Air Force: "Aim High" campaign 119
U.S. Army 119, 128
U.S. Department of Energy 50
"Using Your Positioning for More Reward, Impact, Control, and Fun" (2012 New Business Summit) 31

"Valuation + Succession for the Modern Marketing Firm" 128
VanAuken, Brad 137; "Anatomy of a Marketing Plan" 136
Vimeo 164

Walker, T.J. 62
Wall, Angus 156
websites 161–162
"Website that Works, A" (O'Brien) 63, 66
WeChat 63
Weiss, Alan 26, 40; "Getting Started in Consulting" 25
Wevers, Max 158
WhatsApp 164
"Why Do We Need Presentation Skills" (Andrews) 160
wide news release distribution 59–61
Wilcox, Dennis: "Public Relations Strategies and Tactics" 44–45
Williams, Pharrell 158
WordPress 164
Writer's Market 111, 112

Yes Men 45, 46
YouGov Brand Index 66
YouGov Global Brand Health Rankings (2018) 43
youtility 63, 81
"Youtility" (Baer) 63, 161
YouTube 43, 66, 164

Zaslow, Jeffrey: "Last Lecture, The" 160
Zwilling, Martin 40

Printed in the United States
by Baker & Taylor Publisher Services